The Abiding Cycle

THE ABIDING CYCLE

KNOWING GOD BY EXPERIENCE
THROUGH OBEDIENCE

GLEN WHATLEY

The Abiding Cycle:
Knowing God by Experience through Obedience

A publication of The Gathering Place Press in Alexandria, Louisiana.

Cover design: Alex Felter (felterillustration.com)
Interior design: Benjamin Vrbicek (benjaminvrbicek.com)

Trade Paperback ISBN 13: 978-1-7348436-0-6
Ebook ISBN: 978-1-7348436-1-3

This book would never have been completed without the abiding partnership of my incredible wife, Tylitha, and the support of the incredible network of Gathering Place churches who flesh these truths out daily. Thank you!

To my dad, whose recent passing has reminded me of how much my life is a direct reflection of his love for God.

CONTENTS

INTRODUCTION

I think we are missing the point.
There. I have said it. After thirty-eight years in the ministry, I have finally found enough freedom in Christ to admit it. In our attempts to study the Bible diligently and find truth, I think we have missed the point. In all of our rushing around to *do* something *special* for God, we have become very busy, but we zoomed right past the point of it all. In all of our striving to be better Christians and to have supernatural experiences with God, we have missed the point. In the countless hours of meetings and programs, in the building of tremendous buildings, in the filling of those buildings with people, we have missed it. As a matter of fact, our fixation on these very things might be the reason we are missing the point.

Just take a look at the questions we ask and draw your own conclusions:

How many? How many did your church have in worship this week? How many people has your church baptized this year? How many times have you shared the gospel? How many people came to your church program? How many trips, sermons, small groups,

1

podcasts, prayers, books? How much money, time, effort?

Who do you listen to? What podcasts have been stretching your thinking lately? Which authors do you follow? What do you think about this musician or that song? What kind of preacher do you have? How well does he unpack things? Does he follow the right trends and is he connected to the right networks? Is he gospel-centered, gospel-motivated, gospel-saturated, gospel-captivated, gospel-activated?

Where have you been? Have you made a trip to Haiti to help with the relief efforts? Have you been to Uganda to minister to orphans? Have you gone to any country to dig a water well? What have you done to help the refuges, widows, orphans, the abandoned, and homeless around the world? Are you buying coffee from some developing country? Do you have plans to make an extreme trip to the 10/40 window to share the gospel?

What kind are you? Are you Baptist, Presbyterian, Pentecostal, Catholic? Are you Arminian, Calvinist, reformed, a "five pointer"? Are you traditional, contemporary, formal, casual, seeker-focused, believer-focused? Do you have Sunday school, life groups, support groups, family groups, children's worship, youth worship, family worship?

Where do you stand? Did you attend the pro-life rally and walk across the bridge? Did you hold a picket sign to let the LGBTQ+ community know where you fall? Are you going to the capital to make sure the Ten Commandments are on the courthouse wall? Are you marching, fighting, holding on, sitting in, standing against, rallying for?

All of these questions, and others like them, are questions that I have asked in order to rate the depth of Christianity. These questions have served as a plumb line for the "successful" Christian life. These are the questions we use to check spirituality. They are the queries we have chosen to measure the effectiveness of believers. They are the questions that comprise the modern-day Christian achievement test, and sadly, they are evidence that we missed the point.

A. W. Tozer said, "In our time we have all kinds of status symbols in the Christian church—membership, attendance, pastoral staff, missionary offerings. But there is only one status symbol that should make a Christian congregation genuinely glad. That is to know that our Lord is present, walking in our midst!"[1]

Attempting to live by a list of standards and measuring people based on their accomplishment of those standards, though prevalent in churches, is not the point of the life of a disciple of Christ. Does that sound strange to you? If you are like me, you have learned to make your good works the focus of life. When Jesus walked the earth with his disciples he redefined religion. It was no longer acting according to a list but living life in relationship with the originator of "right" behavior. They lived with him and learned from him. Their old views of right and wrong changed as they watched Jesus live his life. Every second of every day the disciples had "right behavior" redefined by the one with whom they walked. Eating with tax collectors, staying in the home of a former prostitute, questioning the religious leaders, healing on the Sabbath, and standing in defense of a woman caught in the act of adultery were all practices contrary to the religious plumb line of their day.

---

[1] *Tozer For the Christian Leader*, Moody Bible Institute, 2001, compiled by Ron Eggert, October 27 entry.

More significant than having right behavior redefined, they were discovering the truth about God's character and person through each encounter. Their view of God changed dramatically because they walked with Jesus. Can you imagine the disciples' response when they realized that God came not to condemn sinners but to save them? As they walked with Jesus, they discovered that God eats with sinners, touches the unclean, heals sick people, and receives common men as his friends. All of these truths about the character of God were hidden when life was defined by the list.

It's the difference between religion and relationship. Religion is life by the list. Relationship is walking daily with the Holy Spirit. Though most of us are not walking according to the religion of the Pharisees, or even according to the religion of our parents, I think if we honestly evaluate our questions, our modern-day plumb line, we will find that we are walking in religion. Religion is the human default. We can control a list, manage a list, measure a list, accomplish a list. A relationship with the Holy Spirit is subjective, personal, organic, and hard to measure.

Holding on to this type of religion means missing the point. I hope that as we take time to peer into relational discipleship, you will take a careful, introspective look into your motives. The Holy Spirit has awakened my spirit to realize that though I was theologically sound and successful by the list of ministry standards, I was missing the relationship God created me to enjoy. I was missing the creative, outside-the-box ministry opportunities that God had planned. I was explaining away the promptings of the Holy Spirit because they didn't fit the list. Worst of all, I was missing beautiful discoveries of the character of God that would come through abiding in him.

So, what is the point that we are missing? The point is that God created us to abide in him, and not in a new list of standards. He chose us to experience the workings of his Spirit flowing through us every second of every day. He wants us to experience in his Spirit the same things that the twelve disciples experienced in Jesus. He desires for his disciples to adjust to his agenda from moment to moment. He has plans for us that we could never predict. He has life lessons for us that we desperately need. He has fruit that he desires to produce through us. Ultimately, he wants to reveal his glory to us and to a watching world.

In the pages that follow, I have attempted to capture the essence of abiding. In the beginning chapters, we will look at a biblical definition of abiding and see clearly that God's purpose for man to abide has not changed. From the creation of Adam and Eve until today, God has intended to reveal himself through the process of abiding. In addition, we will see how abiding in Christ and producing fruit are part of an organic and cyclic process. When we fixate on knowledge, to-do lists, and emotional experiences, we miss the point. Finally, I will share a few examples of what "abiding" looks like in the life of one modern-day family—mine.

1

ABIDING IN CHRIST: A CYCLIC EXPERIENCE

I f the "point" is that we were created to enjoy an intimate relationship with God and the practical outflow of that relationship is abiding, then abiding in Christ is arguably one of the most significant teachings in Scripture. Even though the terminology is exclusive to John's Gospel and his epistles, the principles of abiding are the practice of all of the major characters in the stories of the Bible. God's purpose is as unchanging as he is.

We will begin our study in the focal text where Jesus defines abiding: John 15. It will become very clear as we study the context of the teachings on abiding that Jesus was revealing not only its significance for the disciples but also its historical and future significance. Take a look at the context of the teaching.

Final Hours

In John 15 Jesus is speaking to his disciples, and it is among the last lessons he will teach them before his crucifixion. Three years before, Jesus carefully chose twelve very unlikely men to be his disciples and designated them as apostles. He spent every day and night teaching them, sharing life with them, answering questions for them, ministering to them, and modeling what it meant to live in an intimate relationship with the Father.

The disciples had shared so many incredible, life-changing moments together. Many of those moments were opportunities that seemed to simply arise out of the day's events, like the healing of the woman with the issue of blood or sharing a sacrilegious meal in the grain fields. The Final Supper and the events of that night, however, seem intentional and purposeful.

First of all, Jesus sent out some of the disciples to find a special place to share the Passover meal. In typical form, Jesus gave a prophetic word about how they would locate the place. They would be met by a man carrying a water jar, follow him to a location, and then tell the master of that house that Jesus asked, "Where is the room that I can share the Passover meal with my disciples?" (Luke 22:11). The location was divinely chosen, revealing that Jesus was setting the stage for an evening of monumental significance.

When they gathered, Jesus began by washing the disciples' feet, a shocking display of servitude that was not even required of Hebrew slaves. This action revealed the type of servant spirit that Jesus possessed and the type of spirit the disciples would be challenged to emulate. The idea of the teacher or master serving his disciples was a counter-cultural, pride-destroying teaching that Jesus taught on numerous occasions, but this display from Jesus had been reserved for his final retreat with his friends.

After sending Judas out to complete his betrayal, Jesus shared a new commandment with them, a commandment reserved for his last hours with his disciples: "Love one another as I have loved you. This will be the way people recognize you as my disciples" (John 13:34–35). Then he made clear what he meant by the statement "as I have loved you" by revealing himself as the Passover Lamb. He told them that because of his great love for them, he would shed his own blood for their sins and for the sins of the world. He would die so they could live. The traditional Passover meal took on a whole new meaning. As they broke bread and drank wine, Jesus changed the symbolism. These elements would be now and forever symbolic of his body that would be broken and his blood that would be shed. A display of servanthood and a redefining of the Passover feast were one-time events in this once-in-a-lifetime evening with Jesus.

It was in the context of this night of special events and teaching that Jesus told the disciples to abide in him. So, the teaching about abiding has tremendous significance because it was part of this divine encounter. It was among the final lessons Jesus gave to his disciples prior to his crucifixion.

What would the Son of God say to his followers in the closing moments of his life? These would be some of the most significant words he had ever spoken. Though all of the teachings of Jesus are true and life changing, the teachings he gave in this setting and at the close of his life, knowing that he would soon be offered up, are especially meaningful. As I have made every attempt to abide in him over the last few years, I can see why.

John Was the Author

Along with this being among Jesus's last lessons, another aspect that makes this teaching about abiding significant is that John wrote about it. John is the "beloved disciple" who is mentioned in the story of the Last Supper. Even though he is the author of the only Gospel that uses that term, there are several events that show that John shared a uniquely intimate relationship with Jesus.

John was a part of what some call the "inner circle." Along with Peter and James, he was there when Jesus raised Jarius's daughter from the dead. He was one of the three who was with Jesus on the mount of transfiguration and who, according to Matthew's Gospel, was taken by Jesus deeper into the garden for prayer prior to his crucifixion.

John was the one to whom Jesus entrusted his mother. While hanging on the cross he looked down and said to his mother, "Behold your son," and to the disciple whom he loved he said, "Behold your mother." John was the first one to the tomb on Easter morning. He was the first to notice the resurrected Christ on the beach in Galilee when Jesus prepared breakfast for the disciples, and he was the one who leaned on Jesus's chest at the supper. It makes since that when we are studying a topic that is tied to a special intimacy with Jesus, John is best equipped to share it.

In addition, the time in which John's gospel was written adds significance. The Gospel of John, though the exact date is disputable, was the last of the four Gospels to be written. This means that John probably had the other three at his disposal and was able to add some of the elements they had not included. He was able to look at the whole of what had been said about Jesus and his message and present a clearer conclusion. So, conceivably, John perused the other three, and being the beloved disciple, noticed that none covered the teaching about the essence of intimacy with Jesus, abiding.

In addition, he had lived longer than any other disciple, so he had spent more time abiding in Christ (the Holy Spirit) and teaching others how to do the same. Those things that he may not have understood in the upper room were clearly understood after living them out for what few would argue was less fifty years.

John was equipped to see the importance of Jesus's teaching about "abiding," and he tried desperately to communicate its meaning and significance. The term "abide" or "abiding" occurs forty times in John's Gospel and eleven times in chapter 15 alone. In addition, it occurs twenty-seven times in his epistles. In all of his writings, John shed some beautiful light on a topic that is one of the most pivotal in Scripture, and I think after this study you will agree.

A third reason this teaching is significant is that abiding is practical. It shows us how to bear fruit and thereby see the glory of God. As we will see in the remainder of this book, the cycle of abiding that Jesus taught and John presented is the key to living life as a disciple. The secrets that Jesus gave the disciples in the upper room were the very secrets to which the Old Testament was pointing. In this very simple lesson, Jesus teaches how we can produce his fruit and reveal his glory. In a time when Christians seem to have a fixation on things that we can produce for our own glory, this lesson is greatly needed.

Abiding in Christ

As I was preaching through what Jesus taught in the upper room, I noticed a pattern or cycle in his lessons on abiding. I was able to see clearly in the Scripture and in my own walk with the Lord a pattern that I would like for you to see also. These thoughts are not complicated. The Scripture itself speaks clearly. As you and I both know, however, Satan tends to keep our eyes blinded from the simplest concepts because they possess such power. Let's look at some of the Scriptures related to abiding and see the abiding cycle.

> Abide in me, and I in you. As the branch cannot bear fruit by itself, unless it abides in the vine, neither can you, unless you abide in me. I am the vine; you are the branches. Whoever abides in me and I in him, he it is

that bears much fruit, for apart from me you can do nothing. (John 15:4–5)

There are some very simple but profound things that we can learn from these verses alone. They are simple because the thoughts are not complicated. They are profound because of their significance to kingdom life. Jesus is the vine. He is the source of all life. He is the one from whom all fruit comes. He is the beginning and the end of anything that is produced in the kingdom of God. Without Jesus nothing of kingdom value comes into being. He must initiate it, produce it, and sustain it.

We are the branches. We can bear no fruit on our own. Though we may think we are independent and can produce eternal results, we cannot. The only way that we can produce any eternal fruit is to remain vitally connected to the Vine. If we do abide in the Vine, we will absolutely produce his fruit. In fact, we will produce *much* fruit! Of course, it is really his fruit produced through us. So, all of our efforts should be to abide in the vine. We should not strain to produce fruit. The process should be natural. We simply abide and fruit is produced.

What Is Abiding?

So, if our role as a disciple of Christ is simply to abide, then what does it mean to abide? The answer to this question was given to John and the other disciples in the upper room. Thankfully, John clearly shares it in his Gospel. In addition, after years of living it out under the power of the Holy Spirit, John also shared personal insights in his epistles.

If you abide in me, and my *words abide in you*, ask whatever you wish, and it will be done for you. By this my Father is glorified, that you bear much fruit and so prove to be my disciples. As the Father has loved me, so have I loved you. Abide in my love. If you *keep my commandments*, you will abide in my love, just as I have kept my Father's commandments and abide in his love. (John 15:7–10, emphasis added)

The clear message that Jesus is giving us here is that abiding in him means abiding in his words, or obeying his commandments. When we obey the commandments of Jesus, we will bear his fruit. This is how the world will know that we are his disciples and how the world will see the glory of God revealed. God's words need to abide in us. They need not only to make their way into our minds but also to be lived out through our lives. For this to be accomplished, we are totally dependent upon Jesus. He must reveal his will and empower us to carry it out. Very simply, abiding is obeying. John reiterates this truth in his epistles.

Let *what you heard from the beginning* abide in you. If what you heard from the beginning abides in you, then you too will abide in the Son and in the Father. (1 John 1:24, emphasis added)

Everyone who goes on ahead and does not *abide in the teaching of Christ*, does not have God. Whoever abides in the teaching has both the Father and the Son. (2 John 9, emphasis added)

Whoever *keeps his commandments abides in God*, and God in him. And by this we know that he abides in us, by the Spirit whom he has given us. (1 John 3:24, emphasis added)

Abiding in the Son is living according to the things that the Son gives us to do. Because Jesus loves us, he reveals to us what we need to do. This is the way that the Father loved Jesus, and this is the way that Jesus loves us.

The Father loved Jesus:

So Jesus said to them, "Truly, truly, I say to you, the Son can do nothing of his own accord, but only what he sees the Father doing. For whatever the Father does, that the Son does likewise. For the Father *loves* the Son and shows him all that he himself is doing. And greater works than these will he show him, so that you may marvel. (John 5:19–20, emphasis added)

Jesus loves us:

You are my friends if you do what I command you. No longer do I call you servants, for the servant does not know what his master is doing; but I have called you friends, for all that I have heard from my Father I have made known to you. (John 15:14–15, emphasis added)

Notice that Jesus not only gets his direction from the Father but also takes no credit for any of his actions. His whole life was literally the Father living through his body. The same is true when we abide in Jesus or the Holy Spirit. Jesus is able to manifest his life through our bodies. We do nothing on our own.

So, abiding in Christ is being totally dependent on the Vine to give us commands in a way that we will understand them. It is being totally dependent on the Vine to empower us to live out those commands. It is total dependence upon the Vine for a life of obedience. All of this will be done by the Vine who loves us and desires for our joy to be made complete.

Fruit

Fruit is what the Vine produces through us. It is not what we produce on our own. Trying to produce fruit on our own is like a branch going to the store to purchase plastic fruit and then somehow adhering the fruit to itself. The fruit may look authentic from a distance, but it has no life running through it. The same is true about any spiritual activity that we create. All of our efforts to produce fruit are dead. They produce dead religion and empty activity, and they fail to reveal the glory of God to the world around us. It may look impressive on the surface, but it has no life in it. We desperately need God's fruit to be produced and revealed.

What is the fruit that God produces? The Bible describes the fruit in several specific ways. The fruit of the Spirit is described in Galatians 5. Paul writes about the fruit of good works in Colossians 1 and fruitful labor in Philippians 1. Converts are described as fruit in Romans 1 and 1 Corinthians 16. Gifts given to the poor are considered fruit in Philippians 4. But, from all of these biblical examples we can also find a more general definition of fruit, one we will use in this book.

First of all, fruit is the activity of God in our lives. We will discuss this in detail in chapter 7, but for now let's look at a quick example. In John 5 Jesus encounters a crippled man at the pool of Bethesda. He gives the man a simple command to obey. Simple, that is, for anyone who is not crippled. It was a command that required the Vine to act. "Take up your bed and walk." At the moment the command was given, the man, totally dependent upon the Vine, obeyed. Then God's activity was seen—the man took up his bed and walked. This activity was obviously not the fruit of a crippled man. It was God's fruit produced through him. Fruit is the activity of God in and through our lives and is a response to our obedience.

Second, fruit is the glory of God revealed through his activity. This is a definition of fruit we don't usually consider, but you will not be able to miss it as we continue to discuss it in further chapters. In John 14:21 Jesus said, "Whoever has my commandments and keeps them, he it is who loves me. And he who loves me will be loved by my Father, and I will love him and manifest myself to him." Jesus promised his disciples that if they would abide in him, that is, keep his commandments, he would manifest "himself" to them. In essence, Jesus said that the fruit of abiding was a deeper revelation of his person.

In the story of the crippled man, what do you think Jesus revealed about himself? Among many things, Jesus revealed that he is loving and that he has power over sickness. Jesus wants us to know him for who he really is. That revelation comes as we express our faith in obedience. This is the ultimate fruit that God produces, the ultimate gift God has for us—the gift that he longs for us to enjoy is his glory. He wants us to see him in his glory and to praise him from full hearts that have experienced his glory.

The Cycle

The beauty of abiding in Jesus is that it is cyclic. This process is an organic cycle. When, in the power of the Holy Spirit, we understand the will of God and in faith choose to obey, he then does incredible things to us and through us and reveals his true character to us. Once we see the truth about his character, we anxiously anticipate his next command because we want to know him more. We know that obedience to the next command will ultimately yield a deeper understanding of who God is.

This is the *abiding cycle*. This biblical cycle holds the potential to reveal in our experience all of the great truths about the God that we say we know. When we learn to abide in Christ, we begin to see life differently. We begin to see ministry in a totally different light, and—most significantly—we begin to know God by experience as he completes his work in us. As we will see in the next chapter, this has been God's purpose from the beginning of time.

For now, let's go back to our introductory questions. Do these questions we ask each other really reflect that we are longing to know Jesus: 1) How many? 2) Who do you listen to? 3) Where have you been? 4) What kind are you? 5) Where do you stand? I hope we can learn to ask ourselves and others better questions in our journey of abiding in Him together.

2

GOD'S PURPOSE FOR MAN:
EXPERIENCING GOD'S GLORY

I n this chapter we will look at how the abiding cycle ex-
presses the purpose for which man was created. During
seminary I was taught always to be acutely aware of the
context of the passage I was preaching or teaching. Typically,
as with most pastors or teachers, I look at the setting, author,
language, societal considerations, and other contextual clues
in the hopes of gaining deeper insight into the meaning of the
passage.

As I was studying the passages on abiding, I applied this
same discipline, but, as hard as it is to believe, there was an
element that I had not considered. It is hard to believe because it would seem as though any man who calls himself a
minister should have started with this one. The one element
that I had not considered was the context of God's general
purpose for mankind. Why did God create man and how does
abiding fit into that purpose? The more I thought about this
question, the more I recognized how the answer would
change how I interpreted not only this passage, but all of
Scripture. It affected me in such a deep way that I would now
say that we should always read the Bible with God's purpose

for humans in the forefront of our minds and make it our first consideration as we pursue accuracy in interpretation.

God Never Changes

First, let's understand something about the character of God that will inform the search for an answer to this question. The Bible is clear that God does not change. Both the Old and New Testaments attest to that fact directly. In Numbers 23 God gave Balaam a message to speak to Balak. As a part of this message, God made clear to Balak that he was unchanging: "God is not man, that he should lie, or a son of man, that he should change his mind. Has he said, and will he not do it? Or has he spoken, and will he not fulfill it?" (Num 23:19).

James encourages dispersed Christians who are facing all forms of persecution to trust in the Lord. God wanted them to know that, regardless of their circumstances, he had not changed: "Every good gift and every perfect gift is from above, coming down from the Father of lights with whom there is no variation or shadow due to change" (Jas 1:17).

These verses express something about the character of God that is evident in the whole of Scripture. God does not change. If we have ever discovered any truth about God's character, it will always be true. Therefore, if we can know the purpose of God, then we can with that knowledge be certain that his purpose has not changed. God's purpose for man at his creation is the same as his purpose today.

The Purpose of God

There is a clear statement about God's purpose for humans in Paul's letter to the church at Ephesus:

> Blessed be the God and Father of our Lord Jesus Christ, who has blessed us in Christ with every spiritual bless- ing in the heavenly places, even as he chose us in him

before the foundation of the world, that we should be holy and blameless before him. In love he predestined us for adoption as sons through Jesus Christ, according to the purpose of his will, to the praise of his glorious grace, with which he has blessed us in the Beloved. In him we have redemption through his blood, the forgiveness of our trespasses, according to the riches of his grace, which he lavished upon us, in all wisdom and insight making known to us the mystery of his will, according to his purpose, which he set forth in Christ as a plan for the fullness of time, to unite all things in him, things in heaven and things on earth. (Eph 1:3–10)

Before we talk about God's purpose as it is revealed in this passage, notice the description regarding the timing of his purpose. Paul wants us to know that God's purpose was set in motion before the foundation of the world. Prior to the events recorded in Genesis, God had this purpose. And since God never changes, his purpose has not changed. When we understand what God's purpose was in his creation, we also understand God's purpose in our day—they are the same.

God's unchanging purpose before the foundation of the world was that we would be holy and blameless in Christ. The key phrase here is "in Christ." God never intended for us to be self-sufficient or to achieve any type of righteousness on our own. His plan was for us to always be found "in Christ." We were created to abide in him and bear his fruit. God placed us "in him" by redeeming us through his blood. Another interpretation of the word "abide" is "remain." God has placed us "in Christ" and his plan for us is to remain in Christ.

Notice that his purpose was also to make us adopted sons and daughters in Christ. God never intended for us to do life without him or to simply obey a list of rules and doctrines. His purpose was for us to share the most intimate relationship a person could share. His purpose was to make us his children in Christ. He wanted us to have the love of a son or daughter for him.

In Christ he also made known to us the mystery of his will, which we must understand in order to obey him and grow in our knowledge of him. Paul carries this thought into Ephesians 2 and then adds a clear statement about how obedience was part of God's original purpose.

> For it is by grace you have been saved, through faith—and this is not from yourselves, it is the gift of God—not by works, so that no one can boast. For we are God's handiwork, created in Christ Jesus to do good works, which God prepared in advance for us to do. (Eph 2:8–10)

God's purpose has been, is, and forever will be for us to know him in Christ. He created us to walk in an intimate relationship with him and to know him progressively through his revelation of himself to us. His plan for accomplishing this is that in Christ we can understand his will and obey him. Ultimately, his purpose in all of this is for us to see the beauty of his glory and praise his name. His purpose has not changed.

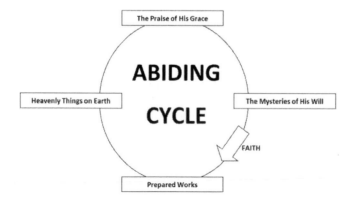

Movement Toward God's Purpose

Since abiding in Christ was God's purpose from the foundation of the world, we can see in the Old Testament narrative how God was moving humanity in that direction. Remember that his purpose was to be fulfilled in Christ, so all that we see in the Old Testament are glimpses of what would finally be accomplished in him. It is interesting to look at the patriarchs and the prophets through the lens of the purpose of God. It has helped me to see how our loving Father has set the stage for us to understand and live in the abiding cycle. Let's take a few familiar stories and show how God's purpose was accomplished.

Noah's Cycle

In the story of Noah, with the purpose of God in mind, it makes sense that God would destroy the whole world because his divine purpose was not being fulfilled. God saw that the intent of humanity's heart was only wickedness. If God's purpose was for man to abide in him, and the whole world apart from Noah and his family was not going to do that, then why wouldn't God destroy the world? He came to Noah, the one man who would abide in him, and gave him a command to follow: "Build an ark, put animals and your family on it, and I will save you." When Noah heard God's plan, it certainly took faith to obey. But Noah was a righteous man who walked in relationship with God. He knew God by experience, and that knowledge informed his decision to obey. After his obedience came God's activity. God sealed the ark, flooded the world, saved Noah and his family, and then caused the waters to recede.

Noah came to know God more deeply through the whole experience. He discovered through the experience that he could actually hear and understand God. He understood to a greater degree the purpose of God for man. He saw the depths of God's love for him. He surely saw the power of God and understood his justice. He came to know God by experience and at the close of this experience, he worshiped.

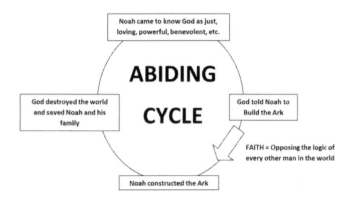

Abraham's Cycle

God commanded Abraham to leave his homeland and move to a place that God would show him. God promised to make his name great. It took faith for Abraham to pack his bags and begin the journey, but Abraham walked in an intimate relationship with God. Without hesitation he took off on a journey with God. Though Abraham doubted in his old age that God would fulfill his promise through Sarah, he never doubted that God would fulfill his promise. Abraham obeyed God, and God gave him as many descendants as the stars in the sky. Abraham came to know God more deeply through God's activity in his life, and Abraham worshiped God.

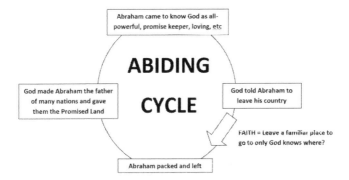

Moses's Cycle

God gave Moses an assignment. God told him to go to Egypt and command Pharaoh to release his people from bondage. Though Moses walked with God, he did not have faith that the people would accept his words. So God did an interesting thing with Moses. He met Moses where his faith was. He told Moses to throw down his staff. That was a command Moses had faith to obey. When he did, he saw God's activity. God turned the staff into a snake. Then God gave Moses a little more difficult command to follow. He told him to pick up the snake. Though Moses was afraid of the snake, he had already learned that God was able to transform it, and he reached out to pick it up. When he did, he saw God's activity. God turned the snake back into a staff. Through his obedience to God's commands, Moses saw God's activity and through God's activity, Moses came to a deeper knowledge of God. This cycle would be repeated over and over again in Moses's life. God gave him many commands to follow as he led Israel, and with each act of obedience Moses grew in his knowledge of God. It is beautiful to see the faith of Moses grow with each trip around the abiding cycle.

In contrast to Moses's experience, let me talk about the Israelites Moses led out of Egypt. Even though God was delivering them out of bondage and walking with them, they were not growing in their faith. They were not coming to know God as Moses was. The reason they were not growing is because they were experiencing God vicariously through Moses. They were talking to Moses and getting their direction from him. So, even though Moses's faith was increased with each act of obedience, Israel's faith remained the same. As Israel faced the Red Sea experience, for instance, the people panicked, but Moses asked God what to do and obeyed. They all walked through the sea together, but only Moses grew. This is evident three days later when the people grumbled against Moses at Marah. They had gained no faith from the Red Sea experience.

A great example of the difference between Moses and Israel is in Exodus 20. When Moses brought the tablets down to the people, God told Moses to invite the people to come near, but notice their response:

> "You speak to us, and we will listen; but do not let God speak to us, lest we die." Moses said to the people, "Do not fear, for God has come to test you, that the fear of him may be before you, that you may not sin." The

people stood far off, while Moses drew near to the thick darkness where God was. (Exod 20:20–21)

The people learned to Moses instead of God. The psalmist may have had this in mind when he observed, "He made known his ways to Moses, his acts to the people of Israel" (Ps 103:7). If we do not draw close to God ourselves to discover his will and allow him to develop our faith to obey, then we will never grow in our knowledge of God by experience. Make a clear note here. You will not come to know God deeply if you are depending on someone else to tell you how to live. Don't let your pastors or leaders deepen their relationships with God while you sit on the sidelines. God wants you to draw near, and if you feel like you are not prepared to do that, hang on and keep reading.

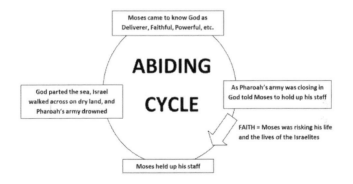

David's Cycle

I love the story of David and Goliath. The Philistine army set up in the valley of Elah, in Israelite territory. Before this battle, the Israelite army had experienced nothing but victory under Saul. But the warriors had no faith of their own. Saul was the one obeying God, and the army was experiencing God vicariously through Saul. In this battle, however, the Lord's anointing had been removed from Saul. So the Israelite army set up for battle and when Goliath stepped out, nobody had the faith necessary to fight him. When David came to bring bread and cheese to his brothers, he heard the defiant cries of Goliath against the God of Israel and immediately God began to stir in him. He knew he would have to fight the uncircumcised Philistine. With the faith that came from numerous experiences with God in the fields, David addressed the giant with a sling shot and God made his shot true. The giant fell.

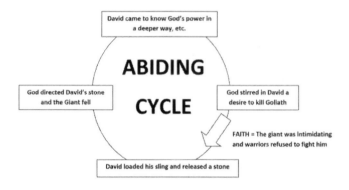

David was as "a man after God's heart." He knew God intimately because he lived in the abiding cycle. David loved the commands and decrees of the Lord (Ps 119). He had experienced God's activity in his life as a shepherd many times. He had defeated lions and bears. His faith was strong because he knew God by experience personally. Though David had some moments of miserable failure as God's king over Israel, he spent most of his reign walking closely with his God. The Israelite people were still following a man, but David was following God and growing in his knowledge of him. David remained the example for all the kings who would follow him. And it was through David's line that Jesus would be born—

one who would never live one second outside the abiding cycle.

These stories are just a few of the many stories of men and women living in the abiding cycle, coming to know God by experience, and pointing to the ultimate fulfillment of the purpose of God in Jesus. I hope that you will take the time to run other stories through the abiding cycle and that God will open your spiritual life up for new discoveries.

The Coming Christ

Throughout the remainder of Israel's history prior to the coming of Jesus, Israel failed to live in the abiding cycle. They refused to come to God to hear his commands. They refused to obey the commands God gave their leaders. They repeatedly did evil in the eyes of the Lord, and as a result, they had no real knowledge of God and never saw his beauty. This was by God's design. God was bringing mankind to ultimate frustration, so people would see their need for Jesus.

During this time God sent prophets to point a frustrated Israel to better days. The prophets spoke of a time when people would see God's glory revealed. They would be empowered to walk with their God. They would have changed hearts and would live in obedience to God and thereby have an opportunity to see his glory. The prophet Ezekiel gives a description of what that day would look like in Ezekiel 36.

> I will sprinkle clean water on you, and you shall be clean
> from all your uncleannesses, and from all your idols I
> will cleanse you. And I will give you a new heart, and a
> new spirit I will put within you. And I will remove the
> heart of stone from your flesh and give you a heart of
> flesh. And I will put my Spirit within you, and cause you
> to walk in my statutes and be careful to obey my rules.
> You shall dwell in the land that I gave to your fathers,

and you shall be my people, and I will be your God.
(Ezek 36:25–29)

The prophet spoke of a time when men would experience
a radical change in their spiritual DNA. God would do some
things that would cause them to have success walking in the
cycle. He said that God would take out their hearts of stone
and give them new hearts. He said that God would wash them
clean and place his Spirit within them. He said that the result
of all of this would be that they would walk in his statutes and
obey him. He told them what would happen as a result of the
redeeming work of Jesus. He told them how in Jesus they
would do what they had only seen a few men and women do
in their history—they would abide in Him. They would be his
people, and he would be their God. This day could not come
soon enough.

Before we leave this chapter, reflect on your own life. The
patriarchs we just read about were dependent on the moment-by-moment leading of God in their lives. Are you taking
advantage of the Spirit's constant leadership in your life?
Most believers today are doing what Israel was doing with
Moses. They are just following a leader. "You talk to God and
tell us what to do." Though their lives may turn out fine, they
are forfeiting countless opportunities for new discoveries of
God in their lives and coming to know God through obedience
is God's purpose for us. Maybe a new question for us to ask
each other is, "Are you seeking God's plan for each situation
in your life?" I think that question does a better job expressing
the essence of abiding than the questions with which we began. So, there you go. One new question to begin to replace
the original five. We are making progress!

3

JESUS AND THE ABIDING CYCLE: OUR PERFECT EXAMPLE

T he Gospels record the life of Jesus. Each narrative tells—from a different perspective—the story of Jesus's daily life and the impact that he had on the. They record his teaching and his miracles, his loving interactions with sinners and intentional dialogue with religious leaders. They each record his ultimate display of love on the cross and his miraculous resurrection. In John's Gospel, however, there is a major focus that the other Gospels only touch, at best: the Jesus's teachings about abiding. Jesus lived in the abiding cycle. Jesus was both the Vine and the perfect branch, the Vine for the disciples and a branch of his heavenly Father.

In the Gospel of John, chapters 5–8 particularly, John records various conversations that Jesus has that demonstrate what it means to live as a branch. Jesus made it very clear that he never acted apart from the Father's prompting. When Jesus obeyed his Father's prompting, the Father did miraculous things through him. Consequently, Jesus came to know the Father by experience as he obeyed. I believe that Jesus came to know the Father perfectly because he never disobeyed. He is our perfect example, and since he is, it is appropriate to look at how he practiced abiding in the Father.

31

Religious Rules and Regulations

> So Jesus said to them, "Truly, truly, I say to you, the Son can do nothing of his own accord, but only what he sees the Father doing. For whatever the Father does, that the Son does likewise. For the Father loves the Son and shows him all that he himself is doing." (John 5:19-20)

As we look at this initial example from John 5, let's first of all look at the inclusiveness of Jesus's statement. He says that he does *nothing* of his own accord. He only does what he sees the Father doing, and because the Father loves him, the Father shows him what he is doing. Jesus takes no credit for anything he does. We will see this in detail through the rest of this chapter, but first recognize the totality of this statement. When we look at the life of Jesus, we need to realize that even though he was the Son of God he received all of his direction from his Father. He lived his whole life in the abiding cycle.

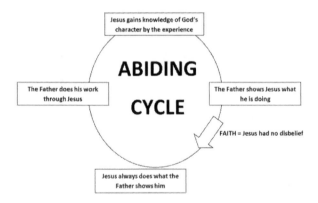

The statements in this passage were not only broad statements about how Jesus remained in the Father, they were also Jesus's response to specific events of the day and in particular, accusations from the Jewish leaders. Earlier that day,

Jesus had healed a crippled man at the pool of Bethesda. He told the man to take up his bed and walk, and since it was the Sabbath, the Jewish leaders were deeply bothered. They were always bothered when Jesus violated their Sabbath rules.

In this instance Jesus was responding to their accusations about his breaking the Sabbath. In essence, Jesus was saying that it wasn't him breaking their rules, but it was his Father. Jesus didn't randomly follow religious rules or hold to religious doctrines. The Father was the one who showed Jesus how to live, and when he led Jesus to live in contradiction to human regulations, regardless of religious pressure, Jesus obeyed his Father.

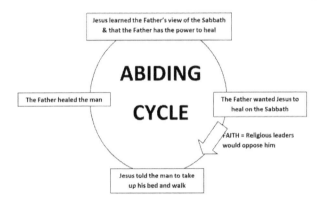

This is such a great example for believers today. I am from the South, and where I live, legalism still runs rampant. There are more denominations than one could imagine in this town, and each church has its own interpretation of how Christians should live. The question that most people are trying to answer is, "Which church is right?" It is confusing to see so many people who all claim to follow Jesus requiring so many different things. Though I certainly do not believe that there are no specific expectations for righteous living that come from God, I do believe that the Holy Spirit should be our source of direction. The Holy Spirit will use people and churches, but ultimately we need to be confident that our actions are a direct reflection of His direction. We only need to act on those divinely inspired directions. My prayer is that God will place you in a church where all that the Holy Spirit leads you to do will be embraced by your brothers and sisters in Christ. In addition, I pray that your church will hold you accountable for releasing any religious practices to which you adhere that are not from the Holy Spirit.

Healing

In this story Jesus came to know his Father's heart not only regarding the Sabbath but also regarding the gift of healing. The Father brought Jesus to this specific man so that he could be healed. What about all of the other people who were sitting by the pools? The Scripture says that there were a multitude of invalids by multiple pools. Why did Jesus offer healing to this one?

He offered healing to one because that is the one the Father showed him. Jesus doesn't perform healing on his own. He looks to see what the Father is doing and whatever the Father does, he does. So in whatever way the father revealed it, Jesus knew that this man was to be healed.

Have you ever wondered why everyone doesn't get healed from sickness even when we pray? There are some who say it is because some formula hasn't been met, like the amount of faith necessary, or lack of elders present, or not addressing the demons correctly. I won't argue those points here, but I will try to draw something from Jesus's example. Jesus didn't do anything except what the Father led him to do. I don't know why the Father didn't heal everyone at the pools, but I know Jesus wasn't interested in a ministry of healing. He was interested in joining the Father in his work.

I would say that by Jesus's example we can conclude that if the Holy Spirit desires to heal someone and involve us, then that person will absolutely be healed. Since the healing begins with the Holy Spirit, He will also bring it to completion. We will discuss this topic in more detail in chapter 7.

Evangelism

> All that the Father gives me will come to me, and whoever comes to me I will never cast out.... No one can come to me unless the Father who sent me draws him. And I will raise him up on the last day. (John 6:37, 44)

Jesus gives a great example here about evangelism. He told a bunch of grumbling Jewish leaders that he was not responsible for drawing people in for salvation. The Jewish leaders to whom Jesus was speaking did not believe. It was not because Jesus didn't make his presentation correctly. It was not because Jesus didn't pray enough prior to this encounter. It was not because he didn't go out with a witnessing partner. Jesus told them plainly that the Father was responsible for drawing people to salvation. They had not been drawn by the Father. Notice that Jesus didn't try to convince them or persuade them. He was completely dependent upon his Father in the ministry of evangelism.

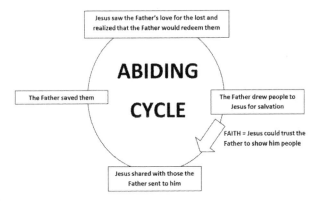

If Jesus depended on his Father to draw the lost, then shouldn't we? I am not saying that we shouldn't share the gospel with people. Jesus certainly called sinners to repentance. I am saying that we need to abide in Christ as we evangelize the lost. We need to put our faith in the Holy Spirit to draw the lost, and then as we are led to share, we must tell what we know. I believe that is what Jesus meant in John 15:26–27:

> But when the Helper comes, whom I will send to you from the Father, the Spirit of truth, who proceeds from the Father, he will bear witness about me. And you also will bear witness, because you have been with me from the beginning.

We need to be sensitive to the Holy Spirit as he works in the lives of people around us. We need to notice when the Holy Spirit has been drawing our lost friends. Then we must bear witness because we have been with Jesus and because we know him. This should not be forced or rushed. We don't have to worry about sealing the deal. Sometimes the strongest act of faith is to wait on the Holy Spirit to do his work. Jesus did evangelism through the abiding cycle, and so should we.

Teaching and Preaching

> About the middle of the feast Jesus went up into the temple and began teaching. The Jews therefore marveled, saying, "How is it that this man has learning, when he has never studied?" So Jesus answered them, "My teaching is not mine, but his who sent me." (John 7:15–16)

I love this passage for a lot of reasons. Of course I love that Jesus's teaching was blowing the minds of the religious leaders. I love that they recognized the power behind the things that he said. I love that he had the ability to teach without having been trained by the "system." But what grabs me most about this passage is that Jesus took no credit for his incredible, life-altering, mind-shattering teaching. Jesus gave the credit for his teaching to the Father. He wasn't pointing to the Father so that he could look humble before the people. He knew that all of his effectiveness in teaching and preaching came from him. The Father gave Jesus the information to teach and empowered him to teach and preach it effectively.

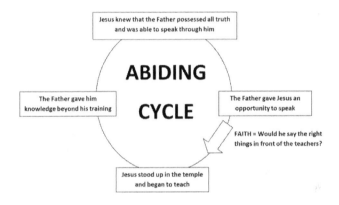

This example of Christ is one that challenges me most. I want to be faithful as a preacher and teacher of the Word of God. There are several considerations that I face regularly that tend to concern me than abiding in Christ. Is the message expository? Am I handling the text properly? Does it have proper form? Is it the right length? Have I put in enough preparation? Are the other pastors and seminary graduates going to agree? There is nothing wrong with these considerations. They are standards to help us preach more clearly and accurately. But are these the standards by which we should measure ourselves?

According to Jesus's example, the most important stand-ard is whether or not we are abiding in the Holy Spirit for our message and our presentation of that message. There is noth-ing wrong with study and preparation, and I believe in seminary education. Don't misunderstand me. I also think, however, that there is very little Holy Spirit anointing on most of our preaching today. God is the one whom people need to hear. He is the one who has the words of life. Somehow our preparation needs to look more like abiding and less like hu-man engineering. I hope you agree.

Authority

> They did not understand that he had been speaking to them about the Father. So Jesus said to them, "When you have lifted up the Son of Man, then you will know that I am he, and that I do nothing on my own authority, but speak just as the Father taught me." (John 8:27–28)

Jesus wanted everyone to know that the authority behind all that he said and did was that of his heavenly Father. Jesus didn't stand on his own authority. He didn't claim any author-ity apart from what was given to him by the Father. Jesus was sent by the Father to do his will. As we have seen in the exam-ples above, Jesus made it perfectly clear that all of the authority behind his every action came from the Father. Jesus lived his life in the abiding cycle. He was God incarnate, and yet, he lived in the abiding cycle.

Why didn't he just claim his own authority as God and live out his life? I believe it was to illustrate for the world what it means to perfectly abide. The disciples watched Jesus live un-der his Father's authority. They couldn't miss it.

We have only touched the surface on how Jesus revealed that he was abiding in the Father. Jesus operated in the abid-ing cycle in regard to his actions (John 5:19–20), his will (John

5:30), his judgment (John 5:30), his testimony (John 5:27, 31), his role (John 6:32–36), his location (John 7:28), his prophecy (John 8:21–28), and even his crucifixion (John 12:27–28).

What a horrible tragedy it would be if we failed to follow his clear example. I hope that you will evaluate why you do all that you do in ministry. Maybe we need to do more abiding. Maybe instead of going to other churches or to books to find ideas for ministry, we need to learn to be more sensitive to the voice of the Holy Spirit. When Jesus spoke about "abiding" in his final hours, the disciples had already seen a perfect illustration of what he meant. He lived his life before them. We have that same person living in us. Let's let Jesus be "all" in our lives and ministry, and through simple surrender, we will gain fresh insights into the magnificence of his person.

4

GOD'S PURPOSE FULFILLED: TRINITARIAN EXPERIENCE

L et's return to the upper room and the Mount of Olives where Jesus taught his disciples about abiding. During these closing moments of his life Jesus tied everything together for them using the "abiding" parable. He drew from how he lived in relationship with the Father and how the disciples lived in relationship to him. Then he pointed them to what life would be like when they would come to abide in the Holy Spirit. They certainly did not understand how all of those things would play out. But, as John had been abiding in the Holy Spirit for fifty-plus years when he wrote his Gospel, we can be certain that he wrote from a clear understanding. I believe his record can help us understand these teachings in their fullness.

So let's put on our "abiding" glasses and take a look at this text. Remember that these are the glasses of biblical context, not preference. All that Jesus taught had its origin in the never changing purpose of God. In addition, it had been lived out in limited form by the patriarchs, and as we have seen, had been perfectly displayed in Jesus's life.

All in a Single Message

In 2012 I preached through the book of John. Taking a year to study and preach through a book means having to keep careful watch on some of the significant elements regarding context. For instance, it took us at least two months to get through preaching the upper room and garden teachings. During that time, I had to constantly remind myself that all of this teaching happened in one evening. What we studied for two months, Jesus taught in a few hours. The disciples were able to tie all of these teachings together much better than we can.

There are some insights that Jesus was trying to communicate to the disciples that evening that will help us seal up some things regarding the concept of "abiding." In these final hours Jesus reminded them of how he had remained in the Father, how the disciples had remained in him, and how eventually they would remain in the Holy Spirit. Take some time to carefully read the following grouping of Scriptures from Jesus's final hours with his disciples and write down what Jesus is saying about abiding.

> Do you not believe that I am in the Father and the Father is in me? The words that I say to you I do not speak on my own authority, but the Father who dwells in me does his works. Believe me that I am in the Father and the Father is in me, or else believe on account of the works themselves.... If you love me, you will keep my commandments. And I will ask the Father, and he will give you another Helper, to be with you forever, even the Spirit of truth, whom the world cannot receive, because it neither sees him nor knows him. You know him, for he dwells with you and will be in you. I will not leave you as orphans; I will come to you. Yet a little while and the world will see me no more, but you will see me. Because I live, you also will live. In that day you will know

that I am in my Father, and you in me, and I in you. . . . I still have many things to say to you, but you cannot bear them now. When the Spirit of truth comes, he will guide you into all the truth, for he will not speak on his own authority, but whatever he hears he will speak, and he will declare to you the things that are to come. He will glorify me, for he will take what is mine and declare it to you. . . . Whoever has my commandments and keeps them, he it is who loves me. And he who loves me will be loved by my Father, and I will love him and manifest myself to him. . . . I am the vine; you are the branches. Whoever abides in me and I in him, he it is that bears much fruit, for apart from me you can do nothing. . . . As the Father has loved me, so have I loved you. Abide in my love. If you keep my commandments, you will abide in my love, just as I have kept my Father's command- ments and abide in his love. These things I have spoken to you, that my joy may be in you, and that your joy may be full. (John 14:10–11, 15–20, 21; 15:5, 9–11; 16:12– 14)

Jesus wanted the disciples to understand that in the same way that he remained in his Father, they had remained and would remain in him, that is, through obedience to his com- mands. The disciples understood what Jesus meant when he said that they could do nothing apart from him. They had ex- perienced failures and successes as they walked with him for three years. Every attempt to do something or be something apart from him brought failure. Every time they simply obeyed what he told them to do, they experienced his power working through them for success. Jesus was teaching them the truth about who he was through the abiding cycle.

Abiding in Jesus

When Jesus fed the five thousand, he began by asking the disciples what they thought should be done. They offered a few of their own thoughts and suggestions, all of which were insufficient. They suggested that Jesus should send the people to the villages to buy themselves something to eat. In response, Jesus told the disciples to give them something to eat. Assuming that Jesus meant for them to purchase food with their own money, they quickly reminded Jesus that they didn't have enough and that they couldn't earn it fast enough. Finally, they either began to understand what Jesus was about to do, or they just made this statement tongue-in-cheek: "We have five loaves and two fishes." Then Jesus revealed himself to them. He gave them an impossible task, then he waited for them to recognize that they were nothing without him and to see the need to offer what they had. Then he blessed the meager meal and gave the disciples commands to follow. He told them to sit the people down in groups of fifty and pass out the food. Jesus could very easily have commanded food to appear before the people, but he gave the disciples an opportunity to abide in him by giving them commands to obey. When they obeyed his commands, the food was multiplied in their own hands.

They could take no credit for the miracle. They simply came to the end of their own abilities and acted on the faith that they had in Jesus. Then everybody was able to see Jesus's activity through the hands of his disciples. The disciples and the rest of the people had an opportunity to come to know the truth about Jesus because the disciples were willing to abide in him. They learned that he was their provider and that he was powerful enough to turn a meal for one person into a meal for five thousand. They learned that he loved people enough to take care of their needs and who knows how many other truths. Because of this experience and others like it, the disciples understood what Jesus meant when he said, "Abide in me, for apart from me you can do nothing."

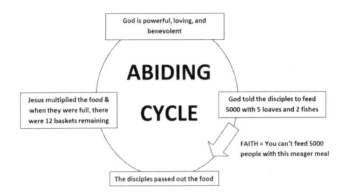

Abiding in the Spirit

Jesus also wanted the disciples to understand that in the way that they had remained in him by obeying his commands, they would remain in the Holy Spirit by obeying the Spirit's commands. Jesus noticed the disciples were troubled when he began to talk about going away. I'm sure they were wondering how they would continue to abide in him if he was not going to be present with them. His comfort to them was that he send the Holy Spirit. They would not only have Jesus living with them, but even better, they would have Jesus living in them (John 14:20). Notice the things that Jesus told them about the Spirit's role in their lives. The Holy Spirit would guide them to all truth. He would take from Jesus all that the disciples needed and give it to them.

All that the disciples needed to continue the abiding cycle would be present in the Holy Spirit. The Holy Spirit would convict them, guide them, and teach them (John 14:26). If they would obey the Holy Spirit's commands, they would see the Holy Spirit's activity. Upon seeing the Holy Spirit's activity, they would come to know deeper truths about the character of Jesus. Jesus told them that the Holy Spirit would reveal things to them that they could not have understood while Jesus was present with them (John 16:12–15).

These promises that Jesus made to the disciples were clearly made manifest at the coming of the Holy Spirit. There is great confirmation of Jesus's teaching about the Holy Spirit in the first few chapters of the book of Acts. The Holy Spirit led believers to do all kinds of different things, and in each event, as they obeyed, the Holy Spirit performed the miraculous. As a result of the Spirit's activity, many people saw the truth about Jesus and placed their faith in him.

Firsts with the Spirit

The most familiar story of the movement of the Holy Spirit is found in the first few verses of Acts 2. This chapter records the coming of the Holy Spirit and gives us the first visible evidence of what Jesus had promised about abiding in the Spirit. Prior to his ascension, Jesus commanded the disciples to remain in Jerusalem until the promised Holy Spirit arrived (Acts 1:4–5). They obeyed what Jesus said, and the Holy Spirit's activity was indeed powerful and life changing.

> When the day of Pentecost arrived, they were all together in one place. And suddenly there came from heaven a sound like a mighty rushing wind, and it filled the entire house where they were sitting. And divided tongues as of fire appeared to them and rested on each one of them. And they were all filled with the Holy Spirit and began to speak in other tongues as the Spirit gave them utterance. (Acts 2:1–4)

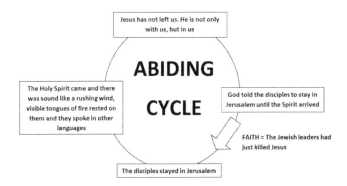

This first time around the abiding cycle with the Holy Spirit is often treated as the only way to experience the Holy Spirit. To limit the Holy Spirit to this first event would be like limiting Jesus to his first miracle. How much would we really know about the character of Jesus if all we ever saw him do was make wine? I think that it would have radically changed Christianity. Christians would all have become winemakers, and the symbol of Christianity would have been a clay pot. Jesus never intended for his followers to fixate on one activity of the Holy Spirit.

In fact, in the following verses of Acts 2 we see the Holy Spirit doing something else. People began to gather around to see what all the commotion was about. As they came near, the disciples continued to do as the Spirit prompted them and spoke. As the disciples spoke, the Holy Spirit touched the ears of those who were hearing them speak.

> And at this sound the multitude came together, and they were bewildered, because each one was hearing them speak in his own language. And they were amazed and astonished, saying, "Are not all these who are speaking Galileans? And how is it that we hear, each of us in his own native language?" (Acts 2:6–8)

This was a second time around the abiding cycle. As the disciples continued to follow the prompting of the Holy Spirit, the people witnessed the Spirit's activity. This time the Spirit translated in each person's language what the disciples were speaking. The result was that the people were amazed and perplexed and began to ask questions. The disciples could see what the Holy Spirit was doing. He was doing what Jesus always did. When Jesus would speak, it was always profound and perplexing, and it always seemed to bring more questions. Then Jesus would reveal truth about himself in his answers. But Jesus was not present in this case, or was he? Who would answer these questions? It was time for the Holy Spirit to guide them again.

> But Peter, standing with the eleven, lifted up his voice and addressed them: "Men of Judea and all who dwell in Jerusalem, let this be known to you, and give ear to my words." (Acts 2:14)

The Holy Spirit now moved Peter to be his voice. This was the same Peter who a few weeks earlier would not admit to a servant girl that he even knew Jesus. He knew the risk that he was taking for making the same proclamation about Jesus that brought about his death, but his faith had been strengthened by these experiences with the Holy Spirit. Jesus was crucified for admitting he was the Christ, and now Peter stood before Jews from every nation under heaven and said, "Let all the house of Israel therefore know for certain that God has made him both Lord and Christ, this Jesus whom you crucified" (Acts 2:36). Peter preached as the Holy Spirit led him. The Holy Spirit filled his mouth and softened the hearts of the people, and they responded to the truth about Jesus.

So those who received his word were baptized, and
there were added that day about three thousand souls.
(Acts 2:41)

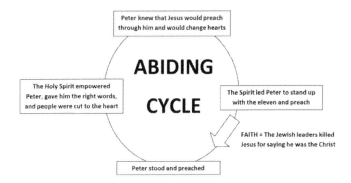

We could go all the way through the book of Acts and see
how the disciples and even new believers who all had received the gift of the Holy Spirit were abiding in the Holy
Spirit and coming to know about the character of Jesus. I rec-
ommend that you take the time to do it.

The Holy Spirit led the new believers to devote themselves to the Apostles' teaching, to fellowship, to the breaking
of bread, and to prayer. They obeyed. The Holy Spirit added
to their number daily those who were being saved (Acts 2:42–
27). The Holy Spirit prompted Peter and John to tell a crippled
man at the temple gate to rise up and walk. They obeyed. The
man began leaping. They came to know the healing power
and the love of the Holy Spirit for the poor and crippled (Acts
3:1–10). With every time around the abiding cycle, these disciples and new believers gained a deeper knowledge of the
truth about Jesus. That knowledge that they gained by experience informed their faith. As they came to know him it
became much easier to obey the commands of the Spirit.

The Apostle Paul

There are so many stories that we could use from Paul's life to illustrate that he operated in the abiding cycle. From the time of his conversion, Paul followed the Holy Spirit's commands, preaching wherever he was told to go. When Paul moved in a direction that he wanted to go, he was often corrected by the Holy Spirit and would adjust to the Spirit's leading. Paul came to know the truth about Jesus as he obeyed in easy times and hard times. His faith grew through his obedience because the Holy Spirit's activity was released in his life. Paul knew Jesus well by experience. He understood how to abide and prayed for the churches that the Holy Spirit started through him. He prayed that they would come to know Christ through abiding. Take a look at his prayer for the church at Colossae and see if you can identify the abiding cycle.

> And so, from the day we heard, we have not ceased to pray for you, asking that you may be filled with the knowledge of his will in all spiritual wisdom and understanding, so as to walk in a manner worthy of the Lord, fully pleasing to him, bearing fruit in every good work and increasing in the knowledge of God. (Col 1:9–10)

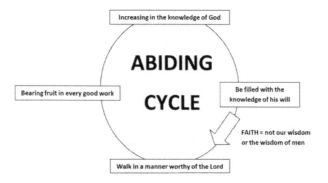

We will share more about Paul's commitment to abiding in chapter 8. For now, I think it is clear that Jesus effectively communicated important secrets during the closing moments of his life. He gave the disciples all that they needed to understand what it meant to abide in him and how to continue after his crucifixion. He drew from how he lived in relationship with the Father and how the disciples lived in relationship to him. Then he pointed them to what life would be like when they would come to abide in the Holy Spirit. When the Holy Spirit came, they saw the complete abiding parable come to life.

We have the same challenge that the disciples had. We need to learn how to abide in the Holy Spirit. We need to learn specific ways to abide in him so that we can continue to grow in our knowledge of the Lord through our experiences with him. In the remaining chapters, we will dive into the details of abiding for believers today. My prayer is that you will gain new insights and begin new practices that will release the Holy Spirit to grow your knowledge of our blessed Lord.

5

ABIDING, STAGE ONE:
UNDERSTANDING GOD'S WILL

I hope it has become clear to you that the abiding cycle is a solid biblical description of what it means to maintain a growing and organic relationship with God. There is no way that we can reduce the vibrant, personal, moment-by-moment relationship that Christ purposed for us to a group of lists. God intends for us to know him by experience as he walks with us every moment of every day. We have allowed numbers, people, buildings, trips, worship styles, politics, and a plethora of other goals to become our definition of what it means to be a good disciple. We have missed the point, but it isn't too late to change.

I believe that there has always been a remnant of people who are hungry to know God by experience in their daily lives. In his book *Pursuit of God*, A. W. Tozer saw these souls as the only visible evidence for true revival of the church.

In this hour of all-but-universal darkness one cheering gleam appears: within the fold of conservative Christianity there are to be found increasing numbers of persons whose religious lives are marked by a growing hunger after God Himself. They are eager for spiritual realities and will not be put off with words, nor will they be content with correct "interpretations" of truth. They are athirst for God, and they will not be satisfied till they have drunk deep at the Fountain of Living Water. This is the only real harbinger of revival which I have been able to detect anywhere on the religious horizon. It may be the cloud the size of a man's hand for which a few saints here and there have been looking. It can result in a resurrection of life for many souls and a recapture of that radiant wonder which should accompany faith in Christ, that wonder which has all but fled the Church of God in our day.[1]

As we continue to flesh out what it means to abide in Christ, my prayer is that you will make a solid decision to be a part of the small cloud. We need revival in the church today and, with Tozer, I am convinced that walking in intimacy with Jesus is the only way it will come about.

A Surprising Word from God

I faced a dilemma during my sixth year of marriage. I didn't feel love for my wife anymore. As a matter of fact, from my perspective there was nothing about her that was loveable. I couldn't remember why I married her. Our son had just been born, and her life consisted of holding him all day long and doing nothing else (again, from my perspective). The house was a mess, meals were not cooked, and she always had a list of things for me to do after I got home from a "long day at the office." As far as attention goes, I wasn't even on her radar, and I resented it. I could only see negative. I was done with her. I was ready to move on.

I didn't want to lose my ministry, so I began to think of how I could be rid of her but also keep my church job. As hard as it is to believe, I began to pray that God would bring another man into her life. I thought that if she committed

---

[1] Tozer, A. W. *The Pursuit of God : (Annotated and illustrated)* (pp. 5-6). Starbooks Classics Publishing. Kindle Edition.

adultery, I might be able to divorce her and remain in the ministry. I even prayed that God would take her life. If she died, I could be above reproach. This stuff probably makes you think poorly of me, and rightfully so. I am choosing to be transparent for a reason.

Even though I was living out what I would describe as a totally selfish life, God met me and revealed his will for me. At that time I was taking a seminary class (I know. . . . hypocritical) that required me to have a daily devotional time and journal what the Lord was saying. On one particular morning God led me to Ephesians 5. I was paying careful attention that morning, not because I was deep spiritually but because it was my turn to share with the class what God said to me through my Bible reading. In verse 25 I read, "Husbands love your wives as Christ loved the church and gave himself up for her." My immediate thought was, "If I had to die for her I would." Then the Holy Spirit brought this thought to my mind, "Really!? You won't even live for her. Why would you die for her?" After pondering that thought, I woke up to the reality of my hypocrisy.

I was convicted. My eyes had been blinded, and I hadn't realized it. I quickly found myself broken and in my brokenness found a desire to repent and to love my wife differently. This new desire was swelling up in me. I meditated on the Word that I had received and came to the clear conclusion that God wanted me to love her selflessly. God wanted me always to give my best to her and never expect anything in return. He wanted me to risk all in loving her. I was challenged and prayed that the Holy Spirit would empower me to do what I knew was God's will. God made his will clear to me. I could not abide in him until he did.

In order to abide in Christ, we must first understand his will. There are many people who have influenced my walk with Jesus through the years. Some I have known personally, and others have impacted my life through their writing. One of the most influential people was Henry Blackaby through his study *Experiencing God*. I know that if you have been through *Experiencing God*, you can see his influence in my writing. I believe Dr. Blackaby was echoing what God was trying to teach the church in earlier generations through men like Charles Spurgeon, Oswald Chambers, A. W. Tozer, George Mueller, and Andrew Murray.

From the late nineteenth century to the early twentieth century, I believe the Holy Spirit was using these men and others to push the modern church into abiding. They saw God as a personal being who longed to walk with humans. They each embraced the leadership of the Holy Spirit in their lives and ministries. They believed that every Christian was redeemed to hear the voice of God and understand his revealed will. They all despised dead religion and saw it robbing the church of an intimate knowledge of God. I believe God used these men to proclaim his never-ending purpose to their generation. Consequently, they stand out to all of us as men who walked with God.

I am so glad to have their examples to draw from and their books to read. People who are thirsty for God need support. Sometimes in the middle of the "list" life, you may feel alone. I hope that what you read here will help you see you are not alone. What you have desired and are desiring can be found in him.

So, what does the abiding cycle look like when it is fleshed out in our generation? I don't claim to have all the answers, but I do hope the remainder of this book will shed some light on what seems to be a growing movement among believers.

Hearing God's Voice

I believe God desires for believers today to know and do his will as much as he has in any other era of human history. As we have seen clearly in the biblical narrative, one of the ways God has always revealed himself is through human obedience. It stands to reason that before we can be obedient to God, we must first know what he desires us to do. Abraham would not have known God as faithful if he had not been given the command to leave his homeland. Moses would not have known God as deliverer if he had not first been given a command to go to Egypt. Jesus would not have known God as savior of the world if he had not first been told to give his himself up as a ransom.

The first step in the abiding cycle is understanding God's will and, more specifically, how God wants us to be involved with him in it. I believe it was clear from the teaching of Jesus that abiding meant understanding and obeying. Specifically, after Pentecost, it means understanding and obeying the Holy Spirit, who is constantly revealing his will to us.

In *Experiencing God* Blackaby says, "God speaks by the Holy Spirit through the Bible, prayer, circumstances, and the church to reveal himself, his purposes, and his ways."[2] I believe this is as true for us as it was for all of the biblical characters we have studied. I believe this is as true for us as it was for our perfect model, Jesus. I believe Blackaby's statement is a good summary statement about how God operates in regard to self-revelation.

God speaks by the Holy Spirit. In this first step of the abiding cycle, let's be totally clear about one thing. We are all completely dependent upon the Holy Spirit to speak to us in a way that we can understand the will of God. We cannot

---

[2] *Experiencing God: Knowing and Doing the Will of God*, Henry Blackaby, LifWay Press, 1990, p.225.

understand the things of God on our own. We cannot do this by simple collaboration with other believers. We cannot do this even by a casual reading of the Scriptures. We need the Holy Spirit. In this first step, as in every step of the abiding cycle, we are totally dependent on the Holy Spirit.

Though most people would agree that the Holy Spirit must guide us, teach us, and lead us, many of these same people are not ever confident that they have ever heard the Holy Spirit's voice. For clarification, when I use the phrase, "heard his voice," I am not speaking of an audible voice. Though some people claim to have heard God speak audibly, and I cannot biblically refute it, most people do not have that experience. We need to get comfortable with the fact that God speaks through the Holy Spirit. We need to learn to recognize the voice of the Holy Spirit if we are ever going to come to know God in deeper ways.

At the time that I am writing this book, I have been married to my wife, Tylitha, for thirty years. I know her voice. If a hundred women were placed on the other side of a curtain and each spoke a phrase, I am confident that I could pick out her voice. I know it by experience. We need to know the voice of the Holy Spirit by experience. Since I have begun to operate in the abiding cycle, I have noticed some patterns in the way God speaks to me. In addition, there are some principles by which I have operated that help boost my confidence that he has spoken.

Principles to Remember

First, God never speaks in contradiction to the inspired, written Word. God has blessed us with a written plumb line regarding truth. When we are wondering whether we have received clear direction from the Holy Spirit, we need to be certain that the word we have received is consistent with biblical teaching. Paul warned Timothy that the time was coming when men would turn their ears away from the truth and gather teachers who would say only what they wanted to hear (2 Tim 4:1–5). He said that the result would be a turning aside to myths. Paul gave Timothy the solution, however, before he ever mentioned the problem: "preach the Word." There is no doubt that many people today are claiming to speak truth and, in fact, are teaching heresy. We need to be watchful regarding false teachers.

For instance, let's say a "pastor" began to gather a group in his home for Bible study. Let's say people enjoyed his teaching and his charismatic personality. They invited their friends, and the friends were equally enamored by this man and particularly enjoyed his twists on traditional theology. Then one day the man shared that he felt like his role as pastor gave him special privileges. One of those privileges was to have multiple wives. If that were not enough, he claims your wife as his own and says that God told him it was alright. Would you believe that God was really the source of his belief? Why not? Because it contradicted the Word of God you would know he was teaching false doctrine.

Erroneous teaching is a very serious problem for the church in our generation, but I believe that there is a far greater problem that exists in the church in regard to abiding. This problem is hindering our discovery of the truth about God. The problem is the paralyzing fear of going the wrong direction. We don't trust that God can speak to us through the Holy Spirit. We constantly waffle between whether it is the Spirit speaking to us or our own desires, and we remain idle. The great tragedy that results from our waffling is that in our failure to move on what we have heard, we forfeit an opportunity to gain deeper knowledge of God through the experience he designed for us. As we have seen in the cyclic process of abiding, forfeiting new knowledge of God also means forfeiting an opportunity to grow in faith. Repeat this cycle over and over again, and we will become a faithless generation. Don't let fear paralyze you.

Second, we need to check our motives regularly. When you are seeking direction from the Holy Spirit, where is your heart? In the abiding cycle, the ultimate fruit we are looking to gain is a deeper knowledge of God. Is that the purpose of your seeking? It is very difficult for us to keep our focus on knowing God. When we are seeking direction, we tend to focus on making the right decision or getting the right result. This is where lists come from. This will often cause us to miss the leading of the Holy Spirit and, as a result, a deeper knowledge of God by experience. So, we need to constantly check our hearts.

This has been a continuing problem for me. I like to think that I am making progress regarding proper motives, but I have such a strong tendency to do whatever will gain the most approval by others. For instance, I enjoy having people comment when a sermon reminds them of a well-known preacher. It makes me feel important and relevant. If I am not careful, though, my goal in preaching will change. I will begin to make my best attempts to sound right or be relevant. I must constantly check my motives in preaching to make sure I am sharing the words given by the Holy Spirit for the purpose of experiencing God in my preaching. Surprisingly, what I have come to know about God through preparation and preaching is that he is both effective and relevant.

Third, we need to keep a child-like faith. Jesus promoted a simple, child-like faith to all who would live in the kingdom of God. When we apply this to the abiding cycle, we need to apply it to our hearing first. If God's ways are higher than our ways and his thoughts are higher than our thoughts, then isn't God going to have to be responsible for communicating his will in a way that we can understand? If I am certain that my heart is longing to know him and that the direction I have received is consistent with Scripture, then I need to act in child-like faith. I need to believe that God has spoken in a way that I can understand and move on to obedience. In my prayers I often tell God, "I am longing to discover more about you through this decision. Whatever I think you are telling me to do, I will do. So, I expect that you will not allow me to think the wrong thing. I am totally dependent on you." I believe that prayer pleases the Father's heart. It has not been a fool-proof method because I have some stubborn flesh, but I am no longer paralyzed in fear regarding God's will and as a result I am coming to know more about my Lord.

Active Listening

In the final chapter of this book I will share some specific stories to clearly illustrate all of the elements of the abiding cycle and how they have worked in my own life. I am always frustrated when I read another person's ideas and don't have any practical examples to clarify them. So, if you are beginning to be frustrated, hang on until the end. In this initial step of understanding God's will there are three active steps we should all consider.

First, as I have already mentioned and will mention again, we must remain dependent upon the Holy Spirit. We must trust him to communicate his will to us in a way that we can understand. We must trust him to speak to us through his Word, circumstances, prayer, and the church. We must remind ourselves of our need for his participation in this element of the cycle.

Second, we need to immerse ourselves in the Bible. My wife and I love to ride our Harley Davidson. We have ridden thousands upon thousands of miles. We have joined the local H.O.G. chapter and received our patches. We have taken and met the challenge of riding 1,000 miles in one day. We have collected pins from Harley shops from coast to coast. We have

Harley clothes, Harley mugs, Harley books, and believe it or not, a 700-square-foot Harley room. We are immersing ourselves in Harley Davidson.

The Bible is God's Word and contains God's plan for our lives. It gives us everything we need know to live in the abiding cycle. It is literally a letter from God to us about who he is, what he is doing, and how we can be a part of his plan. If we really want to know God, i.e., his character, his purpose, and his ways, then we must immerse ourselves in the Bible. We need to read it, hear it, study it, meditate on it, memorize it, teach it, pray it, share it, and, ultimately, act on it.

You don't have to be a Bible scholar to understand the Bible. God designed it so that between your reading and the Holy Spirit's interpretation you can know what it says. One of the main ways that the Holy Spirit will direct you is through the passages that you have encountered from his Word.

When you are asking God about a specific decision in your life and waiting for his answer, make your way to a Bible-teaching church and really listen when the pastor preaches and teachers teach. Pay attention to details when you are reading and studying. Listen to the still, small voice of the Holy Spirit as he brings back Scripture that you have memorized or truths on which you have meditated. There is no better discipline that you could develop as you seek to remain in Christ than immersing yourself in his Word.

Third, learn to be sensitive to the Holy Spirit. Most people can remember a few times when the Holy Spirit clearly spoke to them. They can look back at special moments when they were sensitive and the Holy Spirit highlighted some passage or spoke through a friend. If we are going to abide in the Holy Spirit, however, we need to learn to be sensitive to his voice moment by moment as we walk out our days. Jesus said that it would be better for the disciples if he were to go to the Father so that the Holy Spirit could come. One of the ways that we have it better today is that the Holy Spirit can convict us, judge us, teach us, guide us, and remind us of truth every moment of every day. The Holy Spirit is always speaking to us. We don't have to wait for special moments to hear his voice. He is leading and guiding every second of every day. We simply need to develop a moment-by-moment sensitivity to his voice.

In addition to speaking through the Bible, the Holy Spirit will speak other ways throughout our day. As we are going about our lives, praying without ceasing, the Spirit may prompt our hearts to do something. We may be listening to music, and the Holy Spirit highlights a particular phrase that is applicable to our very particular need. We may be in conversation with a friend and the Holy Spirit uses the dialogue to bring truth to light. We may have been asking a specific question about multiple options available for a decision, and the Holy Spirit removes all options but the right one. We may be on our way to do something, and the Holy Spirit interrupts us in a way that changes our action.

He may speak through the beauty of nature and our enjoyment of it, through billboards, magazines and books, or through dreams and visions. He is not limited in his ability to speak to his children any more than God was limited to speak to Balaam through a donkey (Num 22:28). He can do this because the Holy Spirit is God, and God has not changed. The important thing to remember is that the Holy Spirit is speaking all the time and we need to learn to heighten our sensitivity to his voice. If you feel like you have a hard time hearing, then ask the Lord to help you. Remember that familiarity with his voice happens over time. Each time you hear and obey, you will understand more clearly how he speaks to you.

Fixation

In each of the stages of the abiding cycle there is a danger of fixation. Fixation in this context is when a person or group, having initially experienced the Holy Spirit's power in previous stages of the abiding cycle, refuses to move to the next stage and thereby forfeits the deeper understanding of God that may have been gained. Fixation in any stage always leads to pride, which God hates. When we are stuck in a fixation, the leaders are the people who operate best within that fixation. When people operate in a fixation long enough, they learn how to have mini-revivals within that fixation. Consequently, they quit listening for the voice of the Holy Spirit because they don't need his guidance. They have heard all that they feel they need to hear and have experienced all that they feel they need to experience.

In the first stage of the cycle, we are depending on the Holy Spirit to enlighten us as to the purpose and plan of God. Whenever we study the Word of God and the Holy Spirit enlightens us, we have had a supernatural experience. There is a great deal of satisfaction that comes with the discovery of a new biblical directive. The next step in the abiding cycle is application of or obedience to that directive. Fixation at this stage would be yielding to the temptation to simply seek more understanding, more knowledge, or more directives. This a fixation on "knowing."

There is a very distinct time in my life when I became fixated on "knowing." It was when I first began studying the Bible in college. When I began to take classes in Old Testament and New Testament and got to hear professors open up the Bible in new ways, I loved it! I could not get enough of it! I craved more of it! I could not wait for the next class so the professors could give me more of it.

The problem was I was fixated on *it*, not *him*. I held on to that fixation all the way through my college days and into

seminary. I was proud of what I knew about God and the Bible, and I was quick to reveal my knowledge to others. What
made me a leader in my church was that I was one of the ones
who knew the most. Whenever things started to get dry in my
life, I would just find a book to read that would expand my
knowledge. It would give me a little revival within the fixation. I earned a doctorate from the seminary, but I did not
really know God any better than when I started college.

To this day, there are very few things that I enjoy more
than gaining more knowledge from the Bible about how to
live as a disciple. I do have to be careful, however, to apply
those things that I have discovered. When the Holy Spirit
gives me a new understanding of his will, it is not only so that
I can discuss it and teach it. First of all, it is given so that I can
obey it.

In my church denomination, there have been so many
times that pastors and leaders have allowed themselves to get
sucked into endless discussions about theology. They often
take sides and allow the debate to heighten. These issues are
usually divisions over "disputable matters" (Rom 14:1). The
winner in these debates is the one who knows the most.
Knowledge is king, and if a person can argue his point well, he
owns the kingdom. I really believe that if we were to evaluate
these arguments based on the never-ending purpose of God,
i.e., knowing him through abiding, we might realize our fixation.

Whole churches and denominations can be fixated on academic pursuit. Their pastors wax eloquently from the pulpit
week after week, exposing the beauty of the text from the
original languages and revealing hidden meanings of obscure
passages. They have trained leaders with terminal degrees
leading their Bible studies, and they give awards to laypeople
for hours of study completed. Those who are not theologically
trained will find no place of leadership in these churches.

Their pews are filled with intellectuals who drink in hours of information too lofty for the average person. But nobody is coming to know God by experience because they are fixated on "knowing."

I hope you understand that knowledge of the will of God, provided by the Spirit of God, through the Word of God, is necessary for us to abide in him. By providing a warning about a fixation on "knowing," I am not saying it is not important to know God, his will, and his directives. We are not abiding if we do not gain understanding about those things. I am certain, however, that one of the best tactics of the enemy to keep us from gaining more knowledge of God through experience is to keep everything academic.

I hope that each of us will begin to pursue the will of God more actively. I hope that we will choose to immerse ourselves in the Bible and pay more attention to the prompting of the Holy Spirit that comes throughout the day. I hope that we will be more determined to involve God in decisions we are making by asking for his leadership and waiting for his answer. Both are vital, and both require faith in God. To ask God for guidance and not wait for his answer is not abiding in him. The hardest thing to do is to wait. We must have faith that God will speak by the Holy Spirit and, when he does, we must move quickly to obedience. Then we will find God waiting to reveal himself in wonderful new ways.

6

ABIDING:
OBEYING GOD'S REVEALED WILL

I shared a story in the previous chapter about how the Holy Spirit revealed through the Word my need to love my wife selflessly. In that moment I clearly understood the directive that God had given me and at the same time felt the very real challenge that it brought to my faith. All of my fleshly logic shouted that if I were to practice selfless giving, my wife would take full advantage of me and give nothing in return. That was where our relationship was at that time. I had no evidence to convince me otherwise. I understood on a very small scale what kind of risk Jesus took with humans . . . with me. He gave all with the hope that we would respond to his act of grace.

With the little faith that I had and the strength and encouragement of the Holy Spirit, I chose to make a change. I sat down with my wife one night and asked her to forgive me for not loving her the way that I should have. I shared what the Lord had spoken to me and assured her that I was determined to change as the Holy Spirit would empower me. I made a commitment to attempt to always give and told her that I expected nothing in return. I made a commitment to start that day, and I have been living that way ever since, with only occasional deviations. My obedience released the Holy Spirit to move on my behalf and do what only he could do. It has been a great twenty-four years!

Once we have been given a clear command or directive from the Holy Spirit, the moment for obedience has arrived. Whether or not we obey and the speed with which we obey is determined by our heart and by our faith, both of which are being changed by the Holy Spirit. In Paul's letter to the church at Philippi he encouraged them to work out their salvation through obedience.

> Therefore, my beloved, as you have always obeyed, so now, not only as in my presence but much more in my absence, work out your own salvation with fear and trembling, for it is God who works in you, both to will and to work for his good pleasure. (Phil 2:12–13)

Paul told them that God was working in them both to *will* and to *work*. God is not only taking responsibility for our action but also for the motivation behind our action. God works in us to bring about an authentic internal desire to do his will. He does this by changing our hearts and by growing our faith.

Changing Hearts

In Ezekiel 36 the prophet told of a time when God would remove our hearts of stone and give us hearts of flesh. After we were washed clean by pure water, signifying the blood of Christ, Ezekiel said God would place his Spirit in us and we would be transformed from the inside out. He said the result of this work of God would be that we would walk in his statutes and be careful to obey his rules.

God works in our hearts through our commitment to abide in him. When we discover his will and choose to walk in it, we will gain a deeper revelation of Jesus, and that deeper revelation will affect our hearts every time. Our love deepens for the person whose character has been revealed. Every characteristic that is truly seen during our intercourse with Christ makes him more real to us and more lovable to us. In fact, Jesus said that the reason people don't love him is because they don't obey his commands. "Whoever does not love me does not keep my words" (John 14:21) If a believer keeps his words, he will love Jesus deeply.

This is what God is doing through the abiding cycle. God has transformed your heart. If you could live exactly the way your heart wants to live, you would walk in complete obedience to God. The limiting factor is our flesh. It is the members of our body waging war against our minds (Rom 8). The abiding cycle is the tool that God uses to train our bodies to do what our hearts already desire to do. It is also how he grows our love for him. He is constantly giving us commands to follow that give us the opportunity to know him in deeper ways. Deeper knowledge about God always results in deeper love for God. A deeper love for God always results in a stronger willingness to obey.

The love that God displays to us and the love that we display to him has everything to do with commands and obedience. Jesus told the disciples that if they loved him they would obey his commands and that when they obeyed him, he would love them and reveal himself to them (John 14:21). One of the best displays of Jesus's love for us is to give us commands to follow. Commands come from the heart of Jesus. The best display of love that we can give to Jesus is obedience. Obedience comes from the heart of his disciples. Every act of obedience to the Holy Spirit will result in a greater knowledge and deeper love for him. God uses the abiding cycle to change our hearts so that we will desire to do his will authentically.

Growing Faith

God also works in us to "will" by growing our faith. When the Holy Spirit gives us a command to follow, we will obey immediately if we possess great faith in God. If our faith is weaker, then we will take more time for contemplation or reconsideration, hoping that the Holy Spirit will speak again. If we possess very weak faith, then we may explain away the Holy Spirit's leading altogether. Faith is something we own. It is given to us by God, but we own it (Eph 2:8–9). In the abiding cycle, our faith, or lack thereof, either push us forward into deeper knowledge about God, slow us down, or bring us to a screeching halt. So, faith is an extremely vital element in the cycle.

God does not expect us to dig deeper within ourselves to find more faith. We cannot work harder to create deeper faith in God. I have been guilty in the past of preaching messages that presumed that those listening should be able have more faith simply because I told them they should. I have since come to realize that just as initial faith is a gift from God, any increase in faith is also his doing.

There are two things we need to remember when it comes to faith. First, in the abiding cycle we can do nothing of ourselves. We must abide in him. We must remain totally dependent upon the Holy Spirit to grow our faith so that we can move to obedience. Second, the way that the Holy Spirit grows our faith is by giving us commands to follow that challenge the faith we already possess. Responding in obedience to those commands increases faith.

Remember the story of Moses? God told Moses that he was going to bring Israel out of bondage in Egypt. Moses didn't have faith to believe that God could move the people to listen to him. So, God met Moses at the level of his faith and increased it to prepare him for the task. He revealed his power when Moses obeyed the commands regarding his staff (see chapter 2 above). Prior to this experience Moses had small faith in the power of God. After this experience he packed his bags for Egypt. God grew his faith.

One of the reasons the abiding cycle is cyclic is because of what happens to our faith. Every time God gives us a command to follow and we obey, we see God's activity. When we see God's activity, we come to know God by experience. When we come to know God by experience, we have a much greater certainty about what the Bible says about God. Our faith in the character of God is increased. Once we have experienced God's activity in our lives, the knowledge that we gain about God informs our faith which informs our obedience to his next command. Henry Blackaby says, "We come to know God by experience when we obey his commands and he completes his work in us."[1]

God Working in Me

In chapter 10 I will give numerous examples about how God grows our faith and changes our hearts through the abiding cycle, but let me use one example here to illustrate this work of the Holy Spirit. When I was in seminary the Holy Spirit prompted me once to give $100 to a mission church that my wife and I were visiting. As hard as it may be to believe, we had so little disposable income at the time that I didn't know if we would be able to afford food for the next week. My faith, however, was at such a level that with only a little hesitancy, I trusted God and wrote the check. At the end of the morning service a member of the mission came to me with a gift for us. It was $200! Twice what I had given! We were blown away!

At that moment I recognized that the gift given to us was the result of God's activity. I was grateful for the gift, but I was

---

[1] *Experiencing God: Knowing and Doing the Will of God*, Henry Blackaby, LifWay Press, 1990, p.225.

more grateful for the increased faith that I gained through the experience. When I pondered that God really was my provider, my love for God increased. The next time that the Holy Spirit prompted us to give a monetary gift, our love for God and faith in him as provider had grown, and we didn't even consider whether our needs would be met. We had discovered by previous experience that God was our provider. God worked in us to "will."

Blackaby said, "When you come to a crisis of belief, what you do next tells what you believe about God."[2] This is a revolutionary statement. We need to realize that our reluctance to obey reveals the truth about our level of faith. As believers, we hate to admit that our faith is small. But understanding the abiding cycle can encourage us in such a way that when we recognize that faith is small in an area, we can trust that God will give us challenges that will grow it.

Obedience

I hope we can see a little more clearly how God works in us to "will." When he completes that work in us, the result is always obedience. The beauty of abiding is that God doesn't force us to obey against our wills. He changes our hearts and grows our faith so that we gladly obey. I have grown to strongly resist preaching that attempts to persuade people to obey simply because they should. I have made every attempt to remove words like, "ought," "should," and "supposed" from my preaching. These words tend to communicate a need for disciples to act outside of the Holy Spirit's work in them to "will" (want to). Disciples long to obey. Total dependence on the Holy Spirit means allowing the Holy Spirit to increase that longing by abiding in him.

---

[2] Ibid.

A disciple loves to obey the mandates from the Word of God. When he is immersing himself in the Bible, he is sensitive to the Holy Spirit prompting him to adjust his life to biblical precepts. In addition, he is watchful for the Spirit's prompting throughout his day. When the Spirit gives instruction or direction, it is not an interruption to the disciple's agenda. It *is* the disciple's agenda. He longs to see what the Holy Spirit is doing and how he can adjust to the Holy Spirit's work. Obedience is the natural culmination of the expressions of love and faith that a disciple has for the Lord. Without obedience, faith is not faith and love is not expressed.

In the book of James, the apostle writes about faith and obedience. He asks a question and gives an answer that shows that faith and obedience walk hand in hand. You can't have one without the other. The question he asks is, "What good is it, my brothers, if someone says he has faith but does not have works?" His answer is, "faith by itself, if it does not have works, is dead." Other translations interpret the word "dead" as "useless." When something is dead, it no longer exists. Faith is non-existent where there is no obedience that follows.

His Purpose and His Ways

In *Experiencing God* Blackaby says that God speaks to reveal himself, his purposes, and his ways. I believe we have already seen how God reveals himself, and we will speak more about that in chapter 8. But there is something that we need to mention here that many people tend to neglect in discipleship. There are many times when believers receive a clear word from the Holy Spirit about something they need to do. Then they begin to plan and organize the work using logic, reason, and their own ideas. This is not God's way with his disciples. God loves being involved in the details. When we wait on the

Lord to reveal his ways to us, then we are opening up another opportunity for God to reveal his character to us as well.

Paul had a clear call from Jesus to spread the gospel to the Gentiles and to kings and to the children of Israel (Acts 9:15). He clearly understood God's purpose for his life. Fulfilling God's purpose did not mean that Paul did not remain sensitive to the Holy Spirit for specific guidance. Paul was often redirected by the Holy Spirit as he was going about fulfilling God's purpose.

> And they went through the region of Phrygia and Galatia, having been forbidden by the Holy Spirit to speak the word in Asia. And when they had come up to Mysia, they attempted to go into Bithynia, but the Spirit of Jesus did not allow them. So, passing by Mysia, they went down to Troas. And a vision appeared to Paul in the night: a man of Macedonia was standing there, urging him and saying, "Come over to Macedonia and help us." And when Paul had seen the vision, immediately we sought to go on into Macedonia, concluding that God had called us to preach the gospel to them. (Acts 16:6–10)

Though Paul understood his new purpose in Jesus, he was constantly adjusting to the specific leadership of the Holy Spirit so that God could be glorified. He obeyed the Holy Spirit's promptings, and as a result he knew God. There has never been a man who had a deeper knowledge of the beauty of the Lord or who hungered more for a greater understanding of his character. Knowing God was the purpose of Paul's life, and he refused to miss an opportunity for deeper revelations.

Fixation on "Doing"

Remember that in each of the steps of the abiding cycle there is a danger of fixation. When believers become fixated in a particular step of the cycle, it doesn't mean that they have not experienced God. As a matter of fact, the reason they tend to stay put is because they have experienced God and believe that it was something they did. They believe it is something they can control.

When a disciple has obeyed the directives of the Holy Spirit and as a result has come to know God through his activity, that knowledge should lead him to seek more commands or directives. The enemy would like nothing better than to cause us to fixate on doing the same things over and over again. Logic would say, "If obeying God in a specific way brought a specific result, then if we do the same activity again, we should get the same result." Many churches and denominations follow this logic and ultimately forfeit any new experiences with God.

If Noah would have fixated on "doing," he would have become a boat builder. Moses would have spent his life as a snake handler. David would have remained a shepherd, and Paul would have gone from house to house waiting for God to give him a message through another believer. These may seem to be silly examples, but it is true, and it is exactly what many of us are doing today.

The Holy Spirit has led churches to do all types of creative and effective things throughout the centuries. People have come to know God better through their obedience to his promptings. The tendency, however, has been to continue the "doing," without continuing the seeking. So, churches maintain programs and practices that have no life in them. The leaders in these churches are the ones who are the best at maintaining the activity and who can talk the most people into participating. The people who are the best at praying, tithing, teaching, attending, etc. are the people who are our examples. What happens over time is that people eventually find themselves holding on to traditions that have no life in them. In this fixation, revival happens when people are motivated to follow the rules with greater vigor. Commitments are made to attend more, give more, pray more, and do more.

I know what it is like to be stuck in this fixation. For most of the early years of my ministry I was a proponent of this fixation. I thought that I was promoting true discipleship, but in reality I was promoting modern Pharisaical legalism. I was one of the best at keeping the rules, following the doctrines, and promoting the programs. I had great success in getting more people to follow the fixation. I was asked to lead conferences where I could share my successes with other fixated leaders. I helped them learn how to experience revival within the fixation. I climbed higher and higher, and when I arrived at the top of this fixation ladder, God showed me that I had left him behind.

I hope you understand that obeying the will of God as provided by the Word and the Spirit is necessary to abide in him. By providing a warning about a fixation on "doing," I am not saying it is not important for us to obey God's purpose and his ways. We are not abiding if we do not obey. I am certain, however, that one of the best tactics of the enemy that keeps us from gaining deeper knowledge about God by experience is to convince us to continue operating from some type of list. The questions we asked in the introduction of the book supply a great modern-day list if you are having trouble finding one.

As I close this chapter, my prayer continues to be that we will actively pursue the will of God by immersing ourselves in the Bible and paying more careful attention to the moment-by-moment promptings of the Holy Spirit. I pray that we will be more determined to involve God in decisions we are making by asking for his leadership and waiting for his answers. And when he speaks to us, I pray that we will find our faith equal to the task that he assigns and that we will express love to him through obedience. May God give us all deeper revelations of himself through the abiding cycle.

7

FRUIT:
GOD'S ACTIVITY

G od's never-ending purpose for humanity as described by Jesus in his closing hours with the disciples was to abide in him. We have seen that abiding includes understanding God's will and obeying his commands. In this chapter we will look at how the ageless response of God to man's abiding is to produce fruit. Fruit is not something that we can produce on our own. We are totally dependent upon the Holy Spirit to produce his fruit. Consequently, we cannot take any credit for the fruit that is produced. Fruit is God's big production! In response to our obedience, he has chosen to reveal himself through his God-exclusive activity. So to begin our discussion of fruit, let's take a look at God-exclusive events.

Biblical Examples

In the story of Noah, the obvious God-exclusive events were sealing the ark, flooding the world, and removing the water. But other events that might be less obvious are speaking to Noah, building the ark, and gathering the animals. Noah could not have done those things. They were God-exclusive activities, but because God used Noah some may give Noah credit. I can guarantee you that Noah knew that all of these activities were by the hand of God alone.

In the story of Moses, the obvious God-exclusive events ranged from his speaking through a burning bush, to transforming his staff, and manipulating Pharaoh's heart. God performed miracle after miracle through the hands of Moses as Moses obeyed command after command. There was no doubt that Moses could not part the Red Sea, turn bitter water to sweet, produce food from the clouds or water from a rock. Every event in the exodus story was God-exclusive. God said it would be such in his initial dialog with Moses. Notice that God said *he* was delivering his people.

> Then the LORD said, "I have surely seen the affliction of my people who are in Egypt and have heard their cry because of their taskmasters. I know their sufferings, and I have come down to deliver them out of the hand of the Egyptians and to bring them up out of that land to a good and broad land, a land flowing with milk and honey, to the place of the Canaanites, the Hittites, the Amorites, the Perizzites, the Hivites, and the Jebusites. (Exod 3:7–8)

Throughout the Old Testament narrative we read story after story about how God-exclusive events occurred when men and women obeyed his commands. In the New Testament the same was true. As the apostles followed the leading of the Holy Spirit, they saw God-exclusive events occur. When Peter and John, for instance, told the crippled man at the gate called Beautiful to take up his bed and walk, his healing was a God-exclusive event. When there seemed to be some confusion about who healed him, Peter stood up and addressed the crowd:

Men of Israel, why do you wonder at this, or why do you stare at us, as though by our own power or piety we have made him walk? The God of Abraham, the God of Isaac, and the God of Jacob, the God of our fathers, glorified his servant Jesus, whom you delivered over and denied in the presence of Pilate, when he had decided to release him. But you denied the Holy and Righteous One, and asked for a murderer to be granted to you, and you killed the Author of life, whom God raised from the dead. To this we are witnesses. And his name—by faith in his name—has made this man strong whom you see and know, and the faith that is through Jesus has given the man this perfect health in the presence of you all. (Acts 3:12–16)

The miracles that God performed through Paul's life were numerous. Paul understood, however, that though they were great in number, each one was a God-exclusive event. On one occasion Sergius Paulus, proconsul of Paphos, wanted to hear the word of God, so he summoned Barnabas and Paul. Alongside Sergius Paulus was a magician named Elymas who was opposing their teaching. The Holy Spirit prompted Paul to pronounce blindness on the man. Luke's record of this God-exclusive event reveals clearly that Paul knew from whom it came.

But Saul, who was also called Paul, filled with the Holy Spirit, looked intently at him and said, "You son of the devil, you enemy of all righteousness, full of all deceit and villainy, will you not stop making crooked the straight paths of the Lord? And now, behold, the hand of the Lord is upon you, and you will be blind and unable to see the sun for a time." Immediately mist and darkness fell upon him, and he went about seeking people to lead him by the hand. (Acts 13:9–11)

The passage reveals that Paul made the proclamation because he was filled with the Holy Spirit. They were not his words. Paul made it clear to Elymas that his blindness would be the result of the Lord's hand being on him. The Holy Spirit was working through Paul's life, performing God-exclusive acts and revealing God's power and character.

The Galatian church was struggling with issues related to justification. Some said that justification came from works of the law and others understood that it was from faith in Jesus. In his letter to this church, Paul addressed the issue. His words provided for them and for us a clear summary of his view on exactly how much of his life was God-exclusive.

> I have been crucified with Christ. It is no longer I who live, but Christ who lives in me. And the life I now live in the flesh I live by faith in the Son of God, who loved me and gave himself for me. (Gal 2:20)

Paul wanted the church to understand clearly that all righteousness came from Christ. So, if the Holy Spirit does all of the work, what is our role during this step in the abiding cycle? When it comes to God's activity there are three things that I would propose for us to consider: develop patience, embrace our weakness, and watch for God's revelation of himself to us.

Developing Patience

By nature, humans want to be active. We don't like to sit around and wait for things to happen. We want to take control of situations and decide for ourselves what will be the outcome. Christians are notorious about taking control. The reason why so many of us tend to get fixated on "doing" is because we like control. We like to put our religious activity into a nice, manageable plan and then work the plan. Waiting is not only unnatural, but at times it is seemingly impossible.

Abraham and Sarah were like us. God had promised to make Abraham's name great. He said that Abraham would be the father of a great nation (Genesis 15). God promised Abraham that he would have as many descendants as there were stars in the heavens. But as Abraham and Sarah grew older and older, they began to get impatient. Their impatience resulted in the creation of an alternative plan.

> Now Sarai, Abram's wife, had borne him no children. She had a female Egyptian servant whose name was Hagar. And Sarai said to Abram, "Behold now, the LORD has prevented me from bearing children. Go in to my servant; it may be that I shall obtain children by her." And Abram listened to the voice of Sarai. (Gen 16:1–2)

Abraham and Sarah had great faith in God. God had given them numerous experiences through which he had grown their faith. Yet, in this particular moment when they should have been developing patience, they chose to develop another plan. Their plan ultimately caused dysfunction in the family that led to Abraham losing his son Ishmael forever (Gen 16:21).

When we are waiting on God-exclusive activity we need to seize the opportunity to develop patience. God will absolutely complete what he has started. Once we have received a directive from the Holy Spirit and have obeyed all that he has given us to do, we need to trust him to complete the work.

When we begin to get impatient, the enemy will almost always try to convince us that we have not heard from God or have not obeyed correctly. He will attempt to get us to develop another plan that is more manageable and man-sized. At that point most of us will then take the advice of others, like Abraham did, only to find ourselves in a huge mess.

My suggestion is that when we doubt, let's return to the source of our initial action. Let's go back to God and ask for confirmation. One of the reasons we have the story of Gideon in the Bible is to remind us that God will be faithful to keep us on task regardless of how weak we might be (Judg 6). If God wants us to do something else, then the Holy Spirit will communicate that clearly to us. Until that happens, let's work to develop patience.

Embracing Weakness

This step in the abiding cycle also provides a great opportunity for us to learn to embrace our weakness. Now, I know that weakness is not something most people want to embrace in this world's economy. In the economy of God's kingdom, however, recognized weakness is the beginning of great accomplishments.

In Paul's second letter to the Corinthian church he addressed a problem with some false apostles who were apparently more powerful speakers than him. They were trying to draw the church away from the truth, using their human strengths as the lure. In that context Paul gave the church some great truth on which to hold. That lesson applies here.

> I will boast all the more gladly of my weaknesses, so that the power of Christ may rest upon me. For the sake of Christ, then, I am content with weaknesses, insults, hardships, persecutions, and calamities. For when I am weak, then I am strong. (2 Cor 12:9–10)

Paul recognized that greatest asset for God's work was human weakness. This view of his own insufficiency made him acutely aware that it was God who was working in him and through him. Not only was Paul aware of his weakness, but it was about his weakness that he boasted. He understood that the weaker he appeared before people the more the power of God would rest upon him.

It is always beautiful when God works through one of his servants, but it is spectacular when God works through his most unlikely servants. God used Gideon, the weakest member of the weakest tribe of Israel, to lead the armies of Israel against Midian. God defeated them with a tiny army of 300 men armed with empty jars, torches, and trumpets. God used David, a ruddy young shepherd boy, to defeat a giant who held the mighty army of Israel stalemated for forty days and nights. David defeated the giant wearing no armor and armed with a sling shot.

I believe we should embrace our weaknesses. We need to see our weakness as an opportunity for God to reveal his strength. In all of our churches there are people who boast about their knowledge, talents, degrees, administrative skills, teaching abilities, and a host of other human strengths. I have come to see that those things tend to lead the eyes of men away from God's activity. If we are determined to see God do his work, then we need to see our weaknesses as the backdrop that allows his greatness to be on center stage.

Watch for God's Activity

When we have obeyed all that the Holy Spirit has told us to do, we need to keep watch for God's activity. According to all that we have seen about the purpose of God and how he works, we should be expectant when we have completed our assignment. Our faith waits with expectancy for God to complete his work. We may not know what he will do or how he will accomplish it, but we know enough about God to know that he will act.

It is always exciting to see God-exclusive activity. I love being amazed by God when he does his work. There is nothing more fulfilling to a person who is abiding in Christ than having the opportunity to see the fruit. Most significant to a true disciple, however, is watching to see what God reveals about himself through his activity.

When God led Elijah to take on the prophets of Baal and Asherah on Mount Carmel, he told them to prepare a sacrifice to their gods and then pray for their gods to consume their sacrifice with fire. As Elijah expected, nothing happened. Then it was time for Elijah's God to act. Elijah was so confident in God that he had the people pour twelve huge jars of water on the altar. Imagine how fulfilling it must have been for Elijah when God consumed the sacrifice, the altar, and licked up the water in the trench. Wow! But even more significant was what the people learned about God by seeing his God-exclusive activity.

> And when all the people saw it, they fell on their faces and said, "The LORD, he is God; the LORD, he is God." (1 Kgs 18:39)

Fixation on Experiencing

As with all of the steps in the abiding cycle, we need to watch out for fixation. In this particular case we need to be careful not to fixate on "experiencing." It may sound strange for me to say that we should not get fixated on experiencing God, but hear me out.

People are naturally drawn to the dramatic, phenomenal, unique, and unexpected. That is why all of us have at least a little bit of fascination with magicians and illusionists. People flock to have their minds and senses baffled by the unexplainable. Even though we know it is all smoke and mirrors, we love it. Some of the most-watched reality television shows today follow street illusionists and stuntmen. We are blown away by the fantastic feats and things that are impossible to figure out.

Take that natural tendency and apply it to the Christian experience. We love to see the miraculous. Our emotions draw us to places where we can experience the unexplainable. As mentioned in the previous section of this chapter, when God does the impossible, we need to notice it and take it in completely. It is almost always dramatic, phenomenal, unique, and unexpected. But, fixation on "experiencing" means that we don't move on. Instead of seeking the Holy Spirit's next directive, we end up seeking the same experience we just had over and over again.

In Luke 10 Jesus sends a group of disciples out in pairs to heal the sick and preach about the kingdom of God in all the towns and villages where he was about to go. They obeyed the command of Jesus and went out. When they returned they were sharing with Jesus about how they had experienced his power when they encountered demons. They understood that they had no power of their own, but it seems that they were beginning to fixate on the experience. So Jesus gave them a word about fixation.

> And he said to them, "I saw Satan fall like lightning from heaven. Behold, I have given you authority to tread on serpents and scorpions, and over all the power of the enemy, and nothing shall hurt you. Nevertheless, do not rejoice in this, that the spirits are subject to you, but rejoice that your names are written in heaven." (Luke 10:18–20)

When I was a youth minister I found that youth-camp emotions often caused teenagers to fixate on "experiencing." God would move in a service, and students would legitimately notice his movement. But instead of having a deeper love for God and a stronger faith that resulted in seeking God's next directive, they went on and on about how God moved at camp until the feelings were swallowed up by life. The following year they couldn't wait to go back to the same place in order to have another round of the same experience.

Before we write that experience off to the whims of adolescence, let me remind you that adults do the same thing. When God heals someone of an illness, we are looking for the next healing. When God provides money for someone in miraculous ways, we are looking for the next golden pot. When God touches the church in a service through an anointed song, we want that song sung again. If we experience the Holy Spirit moving through us in any way or we see him doing the impossible through our hands, we want that experience again. In fact, we may limit ourselves to that "gifting" and create a special ministry that requires it. These are all fixations on "experiencing."

There are several problems that surface when we fixate on "experiencing." First, as with the other fixations, pride results. The person considered most spiritual in this fixation is the one who has the most dramatic experiences and the largest number of them. He will feel good about his spirituality when he compares himself to others. The tendency then will be to swell up with spiritual pride and to see his role in the church as training others to have more and better experiences.

When a church is fixated on "experiencing," they desire to repeat the dynamic on a corporate level. The practices of the church are all tied to emotional experiences. The biblical text is interpreted as a formula for getting God to give more dynamic experiences. The focus is internal. Everybody wants something spectacular to happen to them, and they will do almost anything to get it.

The greatest tragedy of this fixation is that those stuck in it forfeit any further discovery of the character of God. In many ways they become like the unrighteous that Paul spoke about in Romans 1:24–25: "Therefore God gave them over in the sinful desires of their hearts ... They ... worshiped and served created things rather than the Creator—who is forever praised."

My hope for each of us continues to be that we will begin to actively pursue the will of God, to immerse ourselves in the Bible, and to pay more careful attention to the moment-by-moment promptings of the Holy Spirit. When we understand what the Holy Spirit desires from us, I pray that we will move quickly to obedience. Our obedience will release God to do incredible, God-exclusive things in and through our lives. As he does, let's develop patience, embrace our weakness, and watch for his special revelations. Finally, I pray that we will enjoy the ultimate fruit that God created us for, the beauty of his character.

8

FRUIT:
GOD'S SELF-REVELATION

A
s we continue to abide in the Holy Spirit, we will ultimately see the final fruit of abiding—God's glory!
In the opening chapters of this book we saw that the
unchanging purpose of God before the foundation of the
world was that we would be found holy and blameless in
Christ. Paul told us that according to his purpose God would
reveal to adopted sons and daughters the mystery of his will
and that we would walk in the works he designed for us to do.
All of this would bring about an understanding of the beauty
of our Father and would result in "the praise of his glorious
grace, with which he has blessed us in the Beloved" (Eph 1:6).

In the parable on "abiding," Jesus made it clear that all of
the activity of the husbandman, the Vine, and the branches
was to produce more fruit. The Holy Spirit is only interested
in fruit production. He wants to reveal to us the truth about
who he is through the abiding cycle. Our sole purpose for
abiding should be to see God's activity in order to know him
by experience. God wants us to see his glory. Though there
are times that he reveals his glory apart from our involve-
ment, his intent is for us to be involved. The best way to see
his glory is to experience it firsthand. Remember that Jesus

said as we obeyed his commandments he would reveal himself to us (John 14:21). My hope for this book from beginning to end is that through understanding the abiding cycle we will gain a progressively deeper understanding of the mind-blowing glory of our Father and that with every understanding we will find ourselves more addicted to him.

Biblical Examples

In chapter 2 we looked briefly at a prophecy of Ezekiel. He said that God would do some things that would cause us to have success walking in the cycle. He said that God would take out our hearts of stone and give us new hearts. He said that God would wash us clean and place his Spirit within us. He said that the result of all of this would be that we would walk in his statutes and obey him. He was describing to Israel what we are now experiencing as a result of the redeeming work of Jesus. Prior to this prophecy Ezekiel made it very clear to Israel why God was going to do this great work: so that Israel and the surrounding nations could know him in his holiness. It was so they could see his glory.

> Therefore say to the house of Israel, "Thus says the Lord God: 'It is not for your sake, O house of Israel, that I am about to act, but for the sake of my holy name, which you have profaned among the nations to which you came. And I will vindicate the holiness of my great name, which has been profaned among the nations, and which you have profaned among them. And the nations will know that I am the LORD, declares the Lord GOD, when through you I vindicate my holiness before their eyes.'" (Ezek 36:22–23)

As strange as it may seem, the vindication of the holiness of his name was not an act of punishment but rather a changing of his people. God knew that we could not come to know him without obedience, so he changed us. Through Jesus he made it possible for us to obey him from our hearts and through that obedience come to know the truth about him. In addition, as we obey him the world around us will come to know the truth about him.

Following the events of the flood in Genesis, Noah knew God by experience. The result was authentic worship (Gen 8:20). Following the parting of the Red Sea, Moses knew God by experience. As a result, he composed a song about the marvelous things he discovered about God. In his song he describes God as strength, song, salvation, man of war, glorious in power, majestic in holiness, awesome in glorious deeds, leader of Israel, and the one who reigns forever and ever.

Following God's work through David to slay Goliath, the Israelite army came to know that God was mighty to save. They chased down the Philistine army and defeated them. Following God's display of power through Elijah on Mount Carmel, the people saw that God was personal, powerful, and worthy of their worship. Elijah's prayer was that the fickle people would know that he was God in Israel. Their response of praise immediately after God's activity was that "they fell on their faces and said, 'The LORD, he is God; the LORD, he is God'" (1 Kings 18:39).

After the events of Pentecost the people gave evidence that they had come to know God through his activity.

Now when they heard this they were cut to the heart, and said to Peter and the rest of the apostles, "Brothers, what shall we do?" [38] And Peter said to them, "Repent and be baptized every one of you in the name of Jesus Christ for the forgiveness of your sins, and you will receive the gift of the Holy Spirit. For the promise is for you and for your children and for all who are far off, everyone whom the Lord our God calls to himself." And

> with many other words he bore witness and continued
> to exhort them, saying, "Save yourselves from this
> crooked generation." So those who received his word
> were baptized, and there were added that day about
> three thousand souls. (Acts 2:37–40)

As these new disciples were filled with the Holy Spirit,
they began immediately to follow the Holy Spirit's leadership.
As a result of their daily obedience to the Holy Spirit's directives, more people began to see the truth about Jesus. The
results were phenomenal. People praised God, and he added
to their number daily those who were being saved (Acts 2:46–
47).When the crippled man from the Beautiful Gate was
healed, he praised God and those who saw what God had done
were "filled with wonder and amazement" (Acts 2:10).

Peter's Call

The prior references were from stories we have already mentioned in the book. I wanted to bring them back in this chapter
to show how people responded to what God revealed about
himself in Scripture. When we get to experience God's activity, we can easily see his glory. In each circumstance in life, as
we abide in him, we have a God-designed opportunity to get
to know the beauty of his character. As you read the stories of
the Bible it is easy to see the way God revealed himself to various people through their obedience to his commands and
how they came to know him through his activity.

One other Bible story that I would like to share is Peter's
call. I want to share this story here because it is one of the best
examples of how God's activity causes us to be caught up in
him. Prior to Peter's encounter with Jesus, he had fished all
night and caught nothing. Peter was washing his nets and was
suddenly surrounded by a crowd of people who were

pressing in to hear Jesus speak. This provided a great opportunity for Jesus to invite Peter for a time around the abiding cycle.

Jesus climbed onto Peter's boat. When that happened, all of the possibilities for Peter to know Jesus by experience were available. Jesus gave Peter a quick and easy command to navigate away from the shore so he could finish teaching the crowd. This allowed Peter the ability to see the power of God displayed through Jesus's teaching. It affected Peter in such a way that he gained faith in the words of Jesus. That completed one time around the abiding cycle. It was a simple act of obedience, but it was intentional on the part of Jesus, and it was necessary preparation for the next command.

Then Jesus told Peter to put out into the deep and let down his nets for a catch. Peter responded by first sharing the faith challenge he was experiencing. Peter's faith challenge came because of his knowledge about fishing and the previous night's failure. Peter was a fisherman by trade. He had spent the evening fishing in all the right places and at the right time. He caught nothing. He had already washed his nets. Fishing logic said to ignore Jesus's command. What Peter does next reveals the level of his faith in Jesus.

Peter responded to Jesus by saying, "Master, we toiled all night and took nothing! But at your word I will let down the nets." His faith was not in his own professional knowledge of fishing. Peter had exhausted that knowledge the night before and caught nothing. Peter placed his faith in Jesus by following his commands to put out into the deep and cast his nets. With that done, Peter had completed all that was necessary for a man to do in the abiding cycle. Then it was time for God's activity.

> And when they had done this, they enclosed a large number of fish, and their nets were breaking. They signaled to their partners in the other boat to come and

help them. And they came and filled both the boats, so that they began to sink. (Luke 5:6–7)

Jesus caused them to catch what was probably the largest catch of fish they had ever seen. In the wake of a night of failure, after using all of a fisherman's wisdom, there was no doubt in Peter's mind that Jesus had done this. So, what did Peter, James, and John come to know about Jesus? What was their response to his activity? They came to know Jesus as Lord and themselves as depraved.

> But when Simon Peter saw it, he fell down at Jesus' knees, saying, "Depart from me, for I am a sinful man, O Lord." For he and all who were with him were astonished at the catch of fish that they had taken, and so also were James and John, sons of Zebedee, who were partners with Simon. And Jesus said to Simon, "Do not be afraid; from now on you will be catching men." (Luke 5:8–10)

I love this story because of the next verse. Peter didn't get fixated on "hearing." He didn't try to gain deeper understanding. He didn't ask where, how, or when to throw the net. Peter didn't get fixated on "doing." He didn't consult with other fishermen to see if they thought his net-throwing form was right or to find out how they thought he should make his cast. He simply obeyed. He didn't get fixated on "experiencing." Though he was very blown away by the catch of fish, his response was not more fishing, but repentance and worship. The most surprising and telling response of Peter in this story, however, is found in verse 11: "And when they had brought their boats to land, they left everything and followed him."

Peter, James, and John didn't ask Jesus to come back the next day to show them where to fish. That would have meant that they were fixated on "experiencing." That would have shown a fixation on one particular aspect of Jesus's character. Instead, they left fishing altogether so that they could come to know more of Jesus by experience. They wanted more trips around the abiding cycle with Jesus. They were addicted to the person they had discovered. They stayed with him for the rest of his life and then walked in obedience to his Spirit for the rest of theirs.

The Blessings of Knowledge by Experience

Once we have obeyed the directives of the Holy Spirit, witnessed his activity, and come to know God by experience, the knowledge that we gain about God is something that cannot be taken away. Let's pretend Peter and the sons of Zebedee ran into some of their friends in the market after their experience with Jesus. Their friends were talking about what they heard about Jesus and shared it with the boys. What they heard was that Jesus was a great teacher, but he had no special powers. Do you think that they could convince Peter, James, and John that this was true? Certainly not! They knew by experience that Jesus had special power. Nothing could ever convince them otherwise. This is one of the incredible blessings that come from abiding in Christ. You know that you know what you know about him.

Another blessing is that it informs our obedience to other commands or directives. Once we have gained knowledge of God through experience, we are ready for the next experience with him. When Jesus asked the fishermen to follow him, they didn't hesitate. They responded by leaving their boats and nets and following him. If Jesus had asked them to give up their fishing prior to this experience, they may have been more reluctant or may have turned him down. Each time around the abiding cycle informs the next by changing our way of thinking. When we discover something about Jesus by experience that we didn't already know, we become hungry to know more. With every new discovery we become more passionate about knowing him. This passion for more knowledge about God will never be satisfied in this life because we cannot know him completely until we see him as he is.

As we mentioned earlier, a final blessing that comes from knowing God by experience is the growth that we experience. Our love and appreciation for God grows with every new discovery. When we come to know God by experience, we will never be disappointed in what we find. Every trait of his personality makes him more attractive to us. In addition, our faith in God grows to a new level. With every discovery we make about God we trust him more to guide us and teach us how to live. So, if our faith is weak, all we need to do is join God in the abiding cycle and all of these blessings will be ours.

Fixation on Knowing God

In all of the previous chapters we have spoken negatively about fixations. In this chapter, however, fixation is the goal. God wants us to become addicted to seeing his glory revealed through our lives. He created us to know him in his fullness and to love him as sons and daughters. Nothing brings greater joy to the Father's heart than when we come to know him by experience. In fact, Jesus said that the reason he told the disciples to abide in him was so that the Father might take joy in them and so that their joy would be made complete (John 15:11).

After the apostle Paul spent a few years abiding in the Holy Spirit, he gained an insatiable desire for a deeper knowledge of God. His ultimate goal was not to preach, win souls, or start churches. It was to know Jesus more deeply, and those tasks assigned to him were ways to accomplish that goal. In summary of all of his life's accomplishments, Paul told the Philippian church that knowing God by experience made everything else look like rubbish:

> Indeed, I count everything as loss because of the surpassing worth of knowing Christ Jesus my Lord. For his sake I have suffered the loss of all things and count them as rubbish, in order that I may gain Christ and be found in him, not having a righteousness of my own that comes from the law, but that which comes through faith in Christ, the righteousness from God that depends on faith—that I may know him and the power of his resurrection, and may share his sufferings, becoming like him in his death, that by any means possible I may attain the resurrection from the dead. (Phil 3:8–11)

I guess a final blessing of a fixation on knowing Jesus by experience is that we begin to see our flesh in a proper perspective. Success in all of the other fixations resulted in pride. In the fixation on "knowing," the one who knows the most is prideful. In the fixation on "doing," the one who does the most is prideful. In the fixation on "experiencing," the one who has the most dynamic experiences with the most repetition is prideful. But Paul was fixated on knowing Jesus by experience, and for the sake of gaining more of Christ, Paul suffered the loss of all things, counting them as rubbish.

My prayer at the close of this chapter is that we will become addicted to knowing Jesus by experience, that we will adjust our lives to his plans and directives in order to gain a never-ending array of beautiful discoveries about the character of our Lord. I pray that what we have learned about abiding in the Holy Spirit will transform the way we do life and ministry (chapter 9). I pray that God will guide us to make the changes necessary to our spiritual lives and that he will break us out of any fixations that may be robbing us of the very purpose for which we were created—abiding in him to the praise of his glory!

9

THE PRACTICE OF ABIDING

I know that most of what we have been discussing up to this point has been mainly abstract. Congratulations to all practitioners for making it to this point. I am one of you and understand the challenge. I am very aware that theories about how to abide in Christ will not bring about the revelation that we are desperate to receive. To remain theoretical would be to fixate on "knowing." So, the remainder of the book will be all about application. In the following chapters I hope that we will discover what abiding in Christ might look like when it is fleshed out in our daily lives.

As I write about the practice of abiding, I clearly understand that I am describing one man's application. There are a few things that I hope you will keep in mind as you read. First, these are not the only ways to abide in Christ. As you apply the abiding cycle to your life, you don't have to make the same applications I make. The beauty of the abiding cycle is that it is organic. There is life in the process, and that life is in the Holy Spirit. If you simply do the things that I do without getting your own clear directives from the Holy Spirit, you will soon find yourself fixated on "doing."

Second, because these chapters reflect my personal practice, I will be writing about things that I have experienced in my walk with the Lord. All of the disciplines of my life were formed in the context of my own practice of abiding in the Holy Spirit. So, I will be sharing from my own perspectives gained through the abiding cycle. I will share my life as a disciple of Christ, which will include my experiences as a husband, father, minister, and friend. I hope that you won't spend too much time evaluating the validity of my discoveries but rather will find motivation to have your own.

Third, I am in a work in progress. The more that I have walked with the Lord, the more I realize how little I know. I was hesitant to write this book because I know that right now I see through a glass dimly. I am encouraged, however, that Jesus chose common men to walk with him. Their theology was constantly changing as they continued to abide in Christ. For instance, as they walked through the grain field on the Sabbath and saw Jesus pick grain, their theology about the Sabbath was changed. Part of the beauty of abiding is no matter how much or how little education or experience we have, we are qualified to abide. All of us are constantly discovering God, and so every disciple's theology is destined to change. I realize there will never be a time when I am qualified to write about God from the perspective of complete understanding. There will also never be a time when you will be able to judge my writing from the perspective of complete understanding. That is, until we see him as he is, and at that point I will do a rewrite.

With those things in mind, understand that this book is the result of my practice of abiding in the Holy Spirit. I wrote this book at this time in this place because of the Holy Spirit's clear directives. I pray that you are reading this book at this time in this place because of his leading as well. My hope is that the following pages will clarify any questions you may have about the abiding cycle and that they will help you see that anyone can abide in Christ.

In my practice of abiding in the Holy Spirit I have experienced three stages. I call them stages because they were progressive for me, but as you will see, they are also perpetual. Once I learned them, I continued to walk in them. I will share at least one story in this chapter to describe how each stage works for me.

Stage One: Moments of Glory

During the early years of my walk with God I would describe my experiences with him as "moments of glory." I did not then understand that God wanted to speak to me and guide me through interaction with the Holy Spirit. God was faithful, however, to reveal himself through God-exclusive activity. In this stage his activity was not based on my obedience. He just chose to reveal himself to me by doing something in my life that I would quickly recognize as his work.

My salvation was a stage-one experience with the Holy Spirit. It was the summer before my senior year in high school. I had grown up as an active church member in my small town, but I was fixated on "doing." I had a pretty good bit of religion, but I did not know God. It was in that context that God revealed himself to me.

That summer, I contracted a rare illness called Legionnaires' Disease. My doctor thought it was pneumonia at first and began to treat me. The treatments did not work. As a matter of fact, the fluid doubled in my lungs while I was being treated with multiple types of antibiotics. Eventually a specialist was called in and made a correct diagnosis.

I thought that it was odd that I contracted this particular illness because in my junior English class, the semester before, I chose a random topic for a writing assignment from a list of topics offered by my teacher. The topic I chose was Legionnaires' Disease. I couldn't remember everything I read, but I believe that the Holy Spirit helped me to remember that

over twenty-five people had died within the first week of con-
tracting the disease. God had my attention.

I began to evaluate my life and my beliefs. The Holy Spirit
led me to pick up a Bible and read 1 John. What is funny is that
as far as I knew I was reading it because I thought it would
earn me points with God. Regardless, the Holy Spirit highlighted 1 John 2:3–4: "And by this we know that we have come
to know him, if we keep his commandments. Whoever says 'I
know him' but does not keep his commandments is a liar, and
the truth is not in him."

The Holy Spirit led me to ask a question and then answered it clearly through the Bible. Because of my knowledge
of Legionnaires' Disease and my fear of the possibility of an
early death, my concerns about eternity were heightened. I
wanted to know if I really knew God. The Holy Spirit revealed
the truth to me about my life: that I had no real desire to keep
his commandments and I didn't know him. I understood my
condition, and after carefully considering how my lifestyle
would be affected, I chose to respond by repenting and receiv-
ing Christ into my life.

My life was radically changed. I came to know the Lord as
real, personal, loving, able to speak to me, and ultimately as
healer. My heart's response to this new knowledge about God
was a desire to know what he wanted me to do next. He was
faithful to give me new directives and has done so ever since.
God came in at step three of the cycle and got me started, and
I've been abiding in him ever since.

In stage one God comes to grab our attention through a
God-exclusive activity. It happens at our salvation, and it happens many times after. Before I really began to pursue God,
the majority of my experiences with God were at stage one. If
you were to ask me about what I knew for certain about God,
it would be knowledge I gained through a few special moments over the span of years. I could tell you what I learned

about him through my salvation, a camp experience, a revival service, healing that a friend experienced, etc. These were real experiences and they revealed legitimate truth about God to which I still hold.

I call this stage one because the experiences were few and far between. I only noticed God in the spectacular and miraculous. I didn't see his daily activity in my life, and I was not listening for the voice of the Holy Spirit. If I had an opportunity to give testimony about what I knew about God, I had to get nostalgic, that is, share something from five or ten years ago. God still reveals himself to me through stage-one experiences. They are a vital source of God-given revelation for me, but there are other ways that I have learned to practice abiding.

Stage Two: Setting the Table

In 1990 I went through the *Experiencing God Workbook* for the first time. God used it greatly in my life. For the first time I began to understand that God wanted to speak to me every day. That was revolutionary for me even though I had been in the ministry for eleven years and had a master's degree from a seminary. Having had mostly stage-one experiences with God up to that point, I was pleasantly surprised that God wanted to give me more encounters with him. One of the changes that occurred in my spiritual life as a result was a more active pursuit of the will of God. I developed disciplines that I have come to characterize as "setting the table" for God.

Setting the table involves doing some things in preparation and anticipation of a word from the Holy Spirit. For me it involves spending time alone with a journal, my Bible, and usually devotional books or other Bible study resources. My goal is not to do in-depth Bible study but rather to communicate with the Holy Spirit. I generally begin by praying and writing down any questions to which I need answers. I write down feelings that I have that I don't understand. I write down concerns that I have for family and friends or issues I may be facing in ministry. Then as I read and pray I pay careful attention to anything the Holy Spirit may highlight as answers to those questions. The Holy Spirit uses this process to prepare me to receive his directives.

When I completed the course work for my doctoral dissertation I was offered a job as a national consultant for a major publishing company. It was a job that I aspired to have for a number of years. I had done contract work for them for at least ten years and was honored to have the opportunity to work with them full time. There was an issue that came up, however, as I prayerfully considered the offer. I had spent five years working only part time, which gave me a great deal of time to spend with my wife and young children. Our family was very close, and I didn't want to put that in jeopardy. The concern came when I discovered that the job would put me on the road a minimum of one hundred days per year. Logic said it wouldn't be good for my family, but I needed a word from the Holy Spirit.

The morning that I was scheduled to give my response I went into my time alone with God. I wrote in my journal, "Lord, do you want me to take this job? You know my concerns about how it will affect my family and no matter how much I would like to take this position, I cherish my family more. I need your wisdom." I was reading two psalms and one proverb each day during that time. When I opened the Psalms for the day I read the following:

> Blessed is everyone who fears the LORD, who walks in his ways! You shall eat the fruit of the labor of your hands; you shall be blessed, and it shall be well with you. Your wife will be like a fruitful vine within your house; your children will be like olive shoots around

your table. Behold, thus shall the man be blessed who fears the LORD. (Ps 128:1–4)

I set the table by asking the questions and sharing my concerns. I was ready for the Holy Spirit to answer me, and he did. He answered very clearly. When I took the job I saw God's activity related to my family. When I was not on the road I was able to go into the office at 6:30 and be home when my kids got home from school. Of the one hundred days on the road, about half of those allowed for my family to be with me at some of the most beautiful conference centers and locations in the country. I learned that God can speak clearly, that he loves me, that he is concerned about my family, that he knows the future, etc., etc.

I always encourage people to figure out how to set the table for God. My way is not the only way, but I have certainly experienced God through this method. My time alone with God is exciting and life giving. I have committed to read the Word devotionally in order to immerse myself in it, but I am amazed how the Lord speaks to specific questions I am asking through what seems to be a random discipline. I am equally amazed at how the Holy Spirit will lead me to read a dated devotional book and the thought given by some random author is exactly what I needed to hear and matches the date of my question. When I attend a worship service I expect that the Holy Spirit will speak through the lyrics of the songs and through the message. Attending the service is setting the table.

Pray about what disciplines the Holy Spirit would have you develop and know that the passionate practice of those disciplines is a way to actively pursue more knowledge about God by experience. He will give directives regardless, but disciplines will heighten your awareness to his voice. Before long you will begin to realize how often he speaks and how easy it is to recognize his voice.

Stage Three: Walking in the Spirit

The longer I have walked in the abiding cycle, the more familiar I have become with how the Lord speaks. After a few years of setting the table for the Holy Spirit, not only did I come to know God through obedience to his many commands and directives, but I also noticed patterns in how he spoke to me. I began to understand more clearly what Jesus meant when he said, "my sheep hear my voice and I know them and they follow me" (John 10:27).

This stage is a little harder to describe, but I believe this story may help us distinguish the difference between stage two and stage three. I have noticed a pattern in the way the Lord speaks to me when he is working in the heart of an unbeliever and wants me involved. When I was on staff as a college-campus minister I had an Australian basketball player call for a meeting. He was a professed atheist who came to our Christian college because he was offered a scholarship. He managed to push away all well-intentioned Christians who attempted to "share" with him. But now, during his final month on campus, he called for an appointment with me. I was curious, to say the least.

He came in confused about something that was going on in his life. He shared how he was losing his desire for an array of sinful activities and was gaining a desire to change his life. He jokingly said, "I have even tried to attend some spiritual events on campus." Then he said, "I don't understand what's going on. What's wrong with me?!"

Now, I know it doesn't take a genius to understand that God was working in him, but this was the first time I had ever felt like the Holy Spirit spoke through an unbeliever to reveal that it was time for me to share the gospel. I shared, and he received Christ. His life was radically transformed.

Since that time, I have had person after person reveal their readiness for the gospel message by the Holy Spirit's prompting. For me, this is walking in the Spirit. When I am speaking with an unbeliever, I am always sensitive to the Holy Spirit's voice through the things they say. I quickly recognize when it is time to share.

Take that experience with the Holy Spirit and reproduce it in many different arenas of life, and you will begin to understand what I label as "walking in the Spirit." In stage one I was usually shocked when I recognized the voice of the Holy Spirit. In stage three I am shocked when the Holy Spirit is not speaking. In stage one when the Holy Spirit spoke it shocked my routine because I was mostly self-directed. In stage three it shocks my routine when I begin to step outside the Holy Spirit's directives because I have developed a pattern of looking for his leading.

As I said earlier, these stages were progressive for me. Maybe you can see the same progression in your experience. Whatever the case, I have greatly benefited from learning to recognize the Holy Spirit's voice. Every time I hear his voice and obey his directives, I come to know him a little better. My craving for more trips around the abiding cycle has caused me to set the table for God and the result has been that the Holy Spirit's voice has become more familiar.

I still find God coming into my life with stage-one experiences. I still practice the daily discipline of setting the table for him to speak. And I am still growing familiar with the way he speaks by recognizing patterns through daily abiding. Through all of this, however, the reason I am listening for his voice is so that I can follow his directives and come to know him through his activity. I desperately want to know God more deeply, and I am so thankful that because he loves me he has given me some handles to hold on to.

STORIES OF ABIDING

I n this chapter I want to share more personal stories that may help you to understand what living in the abiding cycle may look like in the life of one person who is passionate about knowing God by experience. I want to remind you of two things as you read. First, these are my stories about how I have experienced God. These are not the only ways to abide in him. You may not encounter God in the specific ways that I have, but if you abide in the Holy Spirit you will have God-exclusive encounters. Second, one of the most difficult things to maintain in the abiding cycle is a focus on the ultimate goal of knowing God. It took me too long to stop fixating on knowledge gained, disciplines learned, and activity experienced. I still regularly feel a tendency toward fixation. I say that because it takes practice to move all the way through the cycle to see God's self-revelation. In the stories found in this chapter I will share ways that I may have been tempted to fixate on preliminary steps in the cycle.

God as Provider

When the Lord made it clear that my wife and I were to return to seminary to pursue doctoral degrees, we both felt that we had clear directives from the Holy Spirit to move our family to campus. The biggest challenge was leaving the church we were serving and, more specifically, the financial security that it provided. To add stress, I asked the Lord to reveal what I was to do to provide for my family while I was a student and the Holy Spirit clearly gave two assignments that would guarantee no regularly scheduled paycheck. So, we moved our family and had no income we could count on. All we could depend on was what we knew about God from previous experiences which provided enough faith to obey.

We had numerous experiences of abiding in the Holy Spirit over the five years on seminary campus. It didn't take us long to see that in addition to theological training, God was also teaching us about his role as provider. I'll share one story that has remained a fresh reminder of God's character whenever we face financial needs.

We were living at times from day to day regarding finances. God was faithful, but he was not allowing us to have money beyond the immediate needs. About the time we began to feel adjusted to operating that way, we had a whole month with no income. Bills were due and we needed income. God provided two opportunities for me to work, and the money was enough to catch up on our bills. This was an ordinary occurrence. What was not ordinary or expected, however, was the school bill and notice that we received after our money was exhausted. The notice required that we pay our existing bill in full or be disenrolled from school and removed from campus housing. The bill was due in four days.

I reached my limit. I had been living for months like a poor man and had tapped every resource to remain in school. I was tired, and my faith had been stretched to what I felt was its limit. As I laid in my bed feeling anxious and racking my brain for options, the Holy Spirit prompted me to pick up my *Experiencing God Workbook*. I had started reading through the study again and had not touched it for two weeks. My initial response was, "I don't have time to read; I have problems to solve."

Eventually, after I shared the problem with my wife and allowed her time to share in the anxiety, I picked up my book and began reading where I had left off two weeks prior. The very first phrase I read was, "When you come to a crisis of belief, what you do next tells what you believe about God." The Holy Spirit repeated the phrase over and over in my mind, "what you do next, what you do next." What I was doing was freaking out! That was not an accurate description of what I had come to believe about God. My wife and I discussed our belief and agreed that God was able to meet this need without our assistance. We agreed that the Holy Spirit was leading us to pray and tell nobody about our need. We obeyed.

Two mornings later my dad came for a visit. We said nothing about our financial needs. Dad took me to a coffee shop on campus and told me why they had come. He had received some unexpected refund and God prompted him to offer to pay off our school bill. Man, I still get chills telling this story! God met the need without our assistance. We were floored by God's miraculous provision, but I've got to tell you that we were more astonished about what we discovered about God. We learned through that experience that God is our provider. He sometimes provides through earned income and other times through other means, but God is our provider. That knowledge gained by experience has carried us through numerous situations where finances were low and Satan tempted us to doubt. God has never failed to provide. He can't. He is our provider. We are more than satisfied with how he does his job.

Summary: We were in financial need. The Holy Spirit spoke through a phrase in the *Experiencing God Workbook*. He told us to pray and trust in Him to provide for our needs. We obeyed by praying and refusing to tell anyone. God provided through my father's refund check. Through God's activity we came to know God as provider. The temptation was to ask God to continue to provide through gifts from people. That would have been fixation on experiencing. The Holy Spirit helped us to trust in God as provider instead. We praised God, our provider!

God as Faithful

Those of you who have raised teenagers can attest to the fact that there are challenges that come with parenting an adolescent. We are so proud of our children and how they have walked out their own faith, but we experienced those challenges like everyone else. When our son was a junior in high school I was burdened about some of the choices he was making and was bringing my concerns before the Lord daily. I happened to be reading a book about the life of Joseph, Jacob's son, and was learning a great deal about my own failures and how God used them in my life to mold me. Then the Holy Spirit spoke to my heart. I believe the Spirit said that my son was Joseph. As I began to dwell on that thought, I saw the truth of that statement. I believe the Lord guided me to understand that, as was the case with Joseph, my son had received many gifts from the Lord but was using them to build himself up. I believe the Lord wanted me to trust that in the same way that Joseph did, my son would one day be used by God to bring him glory. I believe that the Spirit was also forewarning me that my son would have to suffer in order to become all that God would cause him to become. Finally, I believe that the Spirit wanted me to stop trying to correct his behavior and instead trust the Lord to do his work. I received much comfort from these thoughts, and I was confident that I had heard from God. So, I committed to obey.

Over the next weeks, months, and years, obedience was difficult at times, but I usually acted in faith and kept my mouth shut. When I began to doubt God, he was faithful to remind me that my son was "Joseph." During his senior year I went through a period of doubt, and God provided a great reminder. My son attended a high school that was a magnet school for the performing arts. He was active in choral groups and in theatre. The play that was chosen for the fall semester was *Joseph and the Technicolor Dreamcoat*. Todd auditioned and was cast as "Joseph." The Holy Spirit spoke and I laughed as I was reminded to trust God to take care of my son.

When we brought our son to college for orientation day I was experiencing another season of doubt. I struggled with his attitude that whole day and at the end of the day I had really lost hope. The day closed with a chapel service and the speaker used the story of Joseph as his text. I was again reminded to trust God to take care of my son.

After my son graduated from college he became an Americorp Vista. He called and asked us to pray with him about transferring from one assignment to another. He took the new assignment, and his title was "Community Food Justice Cultivator and National Food Security Coordinator" for the Presbyterian Hunger Program. I laughed out loud when the Holy Spirit connected the dots for me. Joseph and my son ended up with the same job: feeding the people. I worshiped God for his fatherly wisdom and his faithfulness to keep me on track.

Summary: I was frustrated with my teenager's choices. God said to leave him alone and trust that he would guide him and ultimately that he would use him as he did Joseph. God reminded me numerous times so that I would not fail to trust him. God grew my son's faith and placed him in a job where he helps to provide good food for the underprivileged. I learned that God is faithful to do what he promises and that it is best to let him teach me how to be a good father. This knowledge about God has caused me to go to him when I feel frustrated with life and trust him to guide me.

God as Guide

God has been so faithful to guide us to the places that he wants us to serve. When we were praying about making a move from Nashville, Tennessee, to Pineville, Louisiana, I asked my parents to pray with us about the decision. My wife and I had been offered jobs at Louisiana College and were praying for God's guidance. After a few weeks of prayer we felt like God was leading us to move. God seemed to be speaking through so many different ways, and we were ready to make our decision. Then my dad threw a kink in the plans. He told me that after praying further about the move he thought we should stay in Nashville.

Needless to say, I respected my dad's words and my certainty became uncertainty. I needed a clear word from the Holy Spirit about what to do. The time for our decision had arrived, and I was waffling in doubt. So I brought my concern before the Lord again, asking him to speak clearly to us. I assured the Lord that even though I respected my dad, my heart was only for him and that I would obey whatever I understood to be his will. The day for the decision came and as I was spending time alone with the Lord that morning, God spoke.

I was completing a study of the book of Romans and landed that morning in chapter 16. I wrote in my journal that morning, "Lord, I need to know how to take what Dad has said. Were his words your words?" I found my answer in verses 17 and 18: "I urge you, brothers, to watch out for those who cause divisions and put obstacles in your way that are contrary to the teaching you have learned. Keep away from them. For such people are not serving our Lord Christ, but their own appetites."

The Holy Spirit showed me that my dad could not separate his own desire for us to remain in Nashville, the town where he lived, from God's will for us. Dad's word was contrary to what God had already spoken to us. When I shared this with my dad he confirmed that we should make the move. I worshiped God, our faithful guide!

Summary: I was unsure about whether or not we should relocate and take new jobs or follow the advice of my father. I felt that God wanted me to ask him for guidance. I asked God to show us what to do. God gave us clear guidance, and my father confirmed what God said. I came to know God by experience as my leader and guide. He confirmed again that he is interested in the intricate details of my life. My love for him and my faith in him was strengthened. This knowledge about God has caused me to come to him with decision after decision to seek guidance.

God as Comforter

When I was called to pastor the church that I am now serving, they had just gone through a very tough experience. I was reluctant to take the job because there was so much baggage that would have to be dealt with. Not only had the church gone through major turmoil, but I had been fired by the former pastor nine months earlier, and some of the remaining members held skewed perceptions of me that. I took comfort that among the elders were some men I trusted and who agreed with the vision the Lord had given me for ministry. I was particularly close to one of the elders and drew much strength from his daily words of encouragement.

Imagine how I felt when I received a resignation letter from that elder one year later. He was resigning as a small group leader and as an elder. Even though my walk with the Lord had never been any stronger, I was blown away. As I went before the Lord early the next morning, I was desperate to hear what he would say to me. I set the table by asking him about how I should respond to the resignation. What God spoke to me that morning showed me that God is in control.

As I opened my journal, the first thing I noticed was something I copied from *Experiencing God Daily* the day before: "Our heavenly Father knows exactly what we will face today and next week. He is eager for us to experience Him as he provides for us." God wanted me to know that he was aware of what would happen the day before and was eager for me to experience him. I was immediately comforted, and I told the Lord that I was ready to hear his voice.

While I was still sharing this moment with the Lord I received a text from another elder who was also apparently spending the early morning hours with the Lord. He said the Holy Spirit led him to text me Isaiah 45. I immediately went to the text and God confirmed his call on my life and promised his blessings on the ministry of this church. Through that one chapter God gave me all of the following words of encouragement:

1. I am empowering you.
2. I am preparing the way.
3. I will give you souls to harvest.
4. I will minister through you in a way that you will know that it is me and not you.
5. I have prepared you.
6. Your church will touch the world.
7. I have sent your trials and struggles.
8. I will remove those who oppose you.

Then I read that day's devotional from *Experiencing God Daily* and God showed me my sin. "Cleanse your hands and purify your hearts . . . draw near to God and He will draw near to you." I was asking God how to deal with the elder's resignation and God showed me my own sin. I was guilty of depending on men for ministry success instead of trusting God.

At that moment I confessed to God: "I have second-guessed you, Lord—what you have spoken. I have operated in the flesh, not in faith. Cleanse me! I will draw near to you."

The next morning God gave me the answer to the question I had asked. Henry Blackaby shared thoughts from 2 Kings 2:9, where Elijah was taken from Elisha. "If you are mourning the loss of one of your leaders, do not despair. God has another leader, for he will see that His will is carried out." I rejoiced that the Lord was in control and that he took the time to comfort me.

Summary: I lost the leadership and ministry companionship of a trusted elder. I second-guessed my call and God's promises for my ministry. I asked God how to deal with the loss and he showed me my sin. I confessed and God comforted me by reminding me that as long as I remain faithful to his leadership, he would accomplish his work through me. The next day he specifically addressed my concern about losing the leader and comforted me by assuring me he would provide another. I committed to walk out God's vision. I am rejoicing today as I reflect on the fact that God has provided eight elders who are tremendous men of God and who have the same vision for ministry that God has given me. I know by experience that God is in control and that he is comforter.

Religion Redefined

We were poor as dirt when we were in seminary, and so there were very few times we could splurge. When we had extra money, we usually saved it for a rainy day, and New Orleans is a seriously rainy city. If we ever splurged on spending it was usually to provide what we thought would be a life-changing, one-time experience for the family. One such moment arose in our second year. My five-year-old son asked me multiple times to take him to the Aquarium of the Americas in downtown New Orleans. I felt pressure not only to provide an opportunity for him to have the experience so many of his friends were bragging about, but I also felt a need for some father-and-son time. So, we decided it was a good splurge.

When we arrived at the aquarium, I saw the ticket price and had a severe gut check. Should I spend this money? Either conviction or justification spoke. I'm not sure which. The message, however, was clear, "When your son is a teenager and struggling with a plethora of sins, he will remember this special experience. In the moment that some punk is trying to get him to try something illegal or immoral, he will shout out, 'No! My dad took me to the Aquarium of the Americas when I was five.'" Obviously, I'm kidding, but I was hoping for a memorable experience and a more-than-typical bonding time. So, I swallowed hard and bought the tickets.

When we entered the aquarium, I was so glad I made the decision. My son was immediately blown away by the big tanks and large exotic fish. I thought, "It's working! We are making a memory!" Our future relationship is secure! Fifteen minutes in, however, I was looking at a shark tank and didn't realize that Todd was no longer beside me. I looked around at nearby tanks expecting that his heightened expectation had led him to another exotic sea creature in another tank. When I finally found him, he was enjoying himself, but there were no fish involved. He had found a unique little ash tray, the kind you dump cigarette butts into and push a button and they magically drop to the bottom. The magic of the ash tray had stolen away my son!

Our bonding time was over. All that money and all those expectations were gone. To this day, twenty-six years later, my son remembers two things about that experience: 1) the ash trays, and 2) the cool automatic blow dryers we used when we washed his ash filled hands. I paid a high price for a fish-filled bonding experience with my son, and he totally missed the point.

After reading this book and studying abiding, I hope you see that we have all been guilty of doing the same thing with God. He has paid the incredible price of his own Son so that we could be united with him and spend our lives gaining experiential knowledge of his indescribable glory. And he has found his church enamored with ash trays and blow dryers. We have missed the point! Surprisingly, our preoccupation with proper fruit has stolen away our pursuit of the source of fruit; Jesus, himself. It is time for us to return to that for which God created us; knowing him by experience through obedience.

In the introduction I mentioned questions that I believe reveal we have missed the point. In the conclusion I would like to consider some better questions. Consider asking yourself these questions to assess your spiritual health. I think you will agree that these are better standards of true intimacy with Christ.

1. In what specific issues are you pursuing God's will presently?
2. How is your personal daily time with God going? Have you been able to really focus and spend quality time with him daily?
3. What has God told you to do with specific issues you are facing, or how is he guiding decisions you are making? How did he speak specifically?
4. What faith challenges are you facing as you consider God's recent revelation of his will to you?
5. Have you worked through your hinderances to obedience?
6. How have you been doing since you obeyed? How are you doing as you are waiting for God?

7. Have you seen God's activity yet in the things that you obeyed?
8. Tell me what God has done in response to your obedience.
9. What did God reveal to you about his character through this experience of abiding?
10. Fill in the blank. God is _____.
11. How has your life been affected by a deeper understanding of God's character?
12. How has your heart toward God changed over the last week, month, year?
13. Has your faith increased because of experiences you have had with God this week?
14. In what way has your faith changed?
15. How determined are you to pursue God's specific will before you act?
16. How has your resolve to wait on God changed? Why?
17. How is your joy and contentment right now?

These other questions in the same vein are going to help us evaluate how much we are truly pursuing God. Every believer is given a new heart at conversion, and that heart, made of flesh and filled with his Spirit, longs for God himself. Satan works overtime to tempt us to move our God-given affection toward some other goal—any other goal—because he knows it will rob us of the joy and contentment that comes from knowing and loving God. He convinced me to point my passions toward religion and religious activity and convinced me that the pride I was feeling was God's pleasure. It was a sneaky approach. Maybe you got caught too. Wouldn't you agree that is time for us to thwart Satan's schemes and finish our pursuit? I have made the shift in my life, and everything has changed. My personal life, my church life, and my ministry are all radically changed.

My Personal Life

I love God! I mean it! This is no longer a phrase I feel obligated to say simply because I am a pastor. They are not empty words in a worship song. I feel it, and not only when something good happens to me or when I get something I want. As a matter of fact, I can honestly say that my affection for God is finally based on the characteristics of his person that I have discovered since I started abiding. This love is real. It is full. It is what drives my pursuit. It is growing over time and consuming my life. Because of my love for God I am rearranging my schedule, reworking my daily routine, and pursuing his will in every area of life. My personal life has been radically changed by abiding in Christ. My personal religion is now both personal and religious.

I have made a shift from the pursuit of admirable religious activities to a passionate pursuit of God himself. The things that I have discovered about God through abiding have filled me with a deep love for him and faith in him. The deeper I search into the character of God through obedience, the more attractive he becomes to me. I want to know him more than I want anything else in life. Though my religious activity may look the same (quiet time, worship, Bible study, prayer, evangelism, discipleship), my pursuit is totally different. I practice these disciplines gladly because I am going after more of God! It is not enough to be consistent in the practice of disciplines. I must encounter God in them. I know this may not make sense to many, but if you really have begun to abide in him, you will understand.

My Church Life

I have also made a shift in the way I view other believers. I used to judge other believers based on their persistence in religious activity. Now, I long for people to know God whether they are religious or not. I know that if I was super religious and missed the point, other people are missing it too. I really feel a deep desire to help people discover the truth about God. My new aim in life is to lead people to know God by experience through obedience. I have also discovered that my relationships with people who abide in Christ are much deeper than any relationships I have had in the past.

I have the tremendous blessing of doing life with a body of believers called The Gathering Place. In Luke 15:1 we are told, "Now the tax collectors and sinners were all gathering around to hear Jesus." Sinners were drawn to Jesus and were listening to him because of who he was toward them. They found acceptance, love, and forgiveness at his feet. We are those people. We have received his salvation and discovered his grace and we have never left his feet. We remain at his feet listening to his voice. When people go to Jesus for direction and to pursue his will, if they look around, they will find community with others there. They will automatically find themselves in unity with one another there. The Spirit leads them to the same place. I love being the church with people who abide.

When we started The Gathering Place we started with a Bible and an empty slate. God has led us in every endeavor. He has put together a beautiful ministry that is simple and effective. As you would imagine, it is also very biblical. People are open to hearing God's direction, so there are no limits to creativity. We have found that God has ideas that no church around us is implementing. We look to him instead of looking around. Testimonies are vital because they help us get a better handle on how God speaks. Worship is truer because we are all gathered to worship God for the things we have actually discovered about him through the week. Our fellowship is richer because we know we all have the same goal: to obey and to know God. We encourage each other to pursue God's will instead of logic or reason alone. It is a very different corporate experience. My church experience has drastically changed.

My Ministry

Abiding in Christ has also changed the way I minister to our congregation and to individuals in our community. I used to give a lot of advice, that is, I told them what decisions to make in life. When I began to abide in Christ, I realized that if I didn't seek direction from God myself, I would rob myself of intimate personal discoveries of God. When I sought God's will for myself, I discovered how personal and consistent he was to me. His personal touch made me bring more of my life to him for direction and ultimately drew me into a lifestyle of abiding.

So, I don't want to rob anyone else of that opportunity. In my new ministry style, instead of telling people what to do, I send them to the Lord for direction. I encourage them to go meet him and hear from him. I teach them how. Then they come back blown away by their own encounters. God certainly speaks through people and uses me to speak his direction for people at times, but I am careful not to rob people of their own personal encounters with God. I used to pride myself in having the answers, and now I am proud to know the one with the answers and gladly send people to him. That is a major shift for me.

The programs we use and money we spend have also changed dramatically. We don't spend much on ourselves. It is amazing how much less it costs to lead people to know God through personal pursuit. God is the draw and the focus. We are no longer trying to draw people to our church. We are trying to lead people to God. The fruit of that is a rich church. We use our money and human resources to love our community, take care of the needs of our people, and send out missionaries. We are light on staff and bi-vocational in house. Our church buildings have been free or cheap, and we are not concerned about drawing people to the church building. People are drawn to the Lord and his people as we love him. This is again a major shift for me.

Abiding changes religion. Everything has changed for me. My personal religious practices, my church practices, and my ministry are completely different. When the source of life changed, the fruit changed. This is how abiding works. When you abide in Jesus your life radically changes. I am a different person since I began to truly abide. I am praying for you. My life is full of joy and the Lord is taking joy in me (John 15:11). I genuinely desire for each person who reads this book to find the depth of joy I have found. It is life changing. It is life defining. He is life changing and life defining. Abide. Go for it! Let nothing stop your pursuit. You will never be the same.

ACKNOWLEDGMENTS

Thanks to Dr. Russell Meek, author and friend, for editing and overseeing the printing of this book. Without you this book would have never left my computer.

ABOUT THE AUTHOR

The Gathering Place Network was formed after many years of conviction about the state of the modern church in America. Dr. Glen Whatley and a small group of leaders planted the first Gathering Place Church in Pineville, Louisiana in 2007. The goal of the church was to allow God to have access to a group of believers for an experiment in church planting. This small congregation committed to search the Scriptures and follow the leadership of the Holy Spirit to learn how to be a biblical community. God has created something simple and beautiful and has opened doors for this network of churches to plant more churches and send missionaries around the world.

Made in the USA
Columbia, SC
28 May 2020